Earth and Other Planets

MODULE A

Earth and Other Planets

How can you be in two places at once? By taking an armchair tour. In this module, you'll observe Earth from outer space, visit the other planets, and get a new look at your beautiful home. So sit back, relax, and prepare yourself for the trip of a lifetime.

CHAPTER

1 Moving in Space

Can you spin around and around without ever stopping? No way! Yet spinning is just one of the constant movements that Earth makes as it travels through space.

CHAPTER

2 The Solar System

You can't beat this system! The solar system offers an amazing collection of planets, asteroids, and comets, along with lots of extra space.

Effects of Gravity

Moon — Path with no gravity

Moon — Path with gravity

CHAPTER

3 The Blue Planet

We're happy to have the blues.
Unlike the other planets of the solar system, Earth is home to blue sky, blue water, and the many colors of life.

In this module

1

Moving in Space

Discover Activity

How do shadows change?

Tape a black paper shape on a sunny window. Look for its shadow. Think of a way to keep track of the shape and position of this shadow. Look for this shadow every 15 minutes for two hours.

For Discussion

1. How would you explain any changes that occur?

2. How will the shadow look in three hours?

LESSON
1.1 *The Moving Earth*

▶ *Is Earth moving?*

Imagine you're in space. Through the windows of your spaceship you can see millions of distant stars and other points of light. One of the stars looks much larger and brighter because that star is much closer to your spaceship. That star is the sun.

Suddenly you notice that one of the points of light seems to be getting larger. But, it's not really getting larger. It's getting closer. As the point of light gets closer and closer, you can see that it's a solid ball of matter—a planet. And, according to the spaceship's computer, the planet is hurtling through space toward you at more than 100,000 kilometers per hour.

The planet is called Earth. It's big, it's blue, it's beautiful, and it's headed straight for your spaceship! On and on Earth rushes. Then, just when you think that Earth will slam right into you, it zooms by, curving away into the distance. Where is this planet, shown in the picture below, going? Read on and find out!

▼ *Earth moving through space*

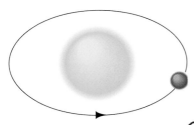

▲ *Earth's orbit around the sun is an ellipse.*

Orbiting the Sun

Earth is going around and around the sun just as a runner goes around and around a track. The path Earth takes as it moves around the sun is called its orbit. The diagram at the left shows Earth's orbit around the sun. Notice in this diagram that Earth's orbit looks like a slightly flattened circle, called an ellipse (i lips′).

Remember how Earth zoomed by your spaceship? Now, imagine you're in the same spot in space one year later. Earth will zoom by you once again. Earth will have traveled almost 1 billion kilometers since the last time you saw it. During that one year, Earth will have made one **revolution** (rev′ ə lü′ shən) around the sun. One full orbit around another object is called one revolution.

Spinning Around an Axis

Revolving around the sun is not the only way Earth is moving. Earth is also spinning. Have you ever spun a toy top? You can learn a lot about Earth's spinning by looking at a toy top. The simplest top looks like a little ball, with a stem on the top side and a sharp point on the bottom. To spin the top you first rest the point on the floor and hold the stem with your fingers. Then you quickly twist the stem and let go. The top spins around and around until it stops.

Now imagine a straight line that starts at the stem of the top, passes through the ball, and ends at the sharp point. That imaginary line is called an axis. The top spins around and around its axis. One full spin around the axis is called a **rotation** (rō tā′ shən). The top makes hundreds of rotations in less than a minute.

Just like a top, Earth spins around and around an imaginary axis. Earth's axis starts at the north pole, passes through the center of the earth, and stops at the south pole. Unlike a top, however, Earth isn't spinning on a solid floor. You can see in the pictures that Earth is spinning in space as it orbits the sun. And unlike a top, Earth never stops spinning. Year after year Earth keeps spinning around its axis.

In the Discover Activity you saw how a shadow moves in a curved path in daylight. The shadow moves because of Earth's rotation. The amount of time for one rotation is called a day. On Earth, one rotation takes 24 hours. Every day of your life, Earth rotates once around its axis. In just over 365 days, Earth makes one revolution around the sun. During all that time, Earth keeps rotating as it orbits the sun.

◄ As Earth revolves around the sun, it also rotates around its axis.

Checkpoint

1. Describe Earth's movement around the sun. What name is given to this pattern of movement?
2. How does Earth move like a toy top?
3. **Take Action!** Have a friend represent the sun and you represent Earth. Show how Earth rotates around its axis while it revolves around the sun.

Activity

Exploring Motion Near the Earth's Surface

When objects fall, they move toward the earth's surface. In this activity, you use marbles to observe how objects move as they get close to the earth's surface.

Picture A

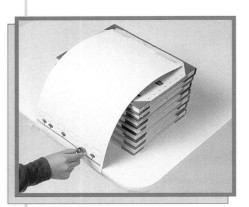

Picture B

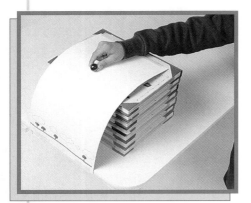

Picture C

Gather These Materials

marker
long piece of
  posterboard, about
  40 cm x 25 cm

stack of books, about
  30 cm high
masking tape
marble

Follow This Procedure

1 Make a chart like the one on the next page. Record your observations in your chart.

2 Use a marker to draw the earth's horizon and some clouds near the bottom of one of the narrow edges of the posterboard. This will represent the area near the earth's surface.

3 Place the stack of books on the table behind the posterboard. Bend the posterboard so that it makes a smooth curve. Tape the top end of the posterboard to the top book in the pile. Tape the bottom end of the posterboard to the table. (Picture A)

> **Predict: *Where along the cardboard will the marble take the longest time to fall?***

4 Hold the marble against the posterboard where you have drawn clouds. (Picture B) Release it. Observe how the marble moves. Record what you observe.

5 Hold the marble against the center of the posterboard. Release it and observe how it moves. Record your observations.

6 Hold the marble near the top of the posterboard and then release it. (Picture C) Record your observations.

Distance from Earth	Effect of Gravity
Earth's horizon	
Above the horizon	
In space	

State Your Conclusions

1. From what point along the posterboard does the marble's speed seem to be the fastest?

2. From what point along the posterboard does the marble's speed seem to be the slowest?

Let's Experiment

How difficult is it to launch a rocket from the earth's surface? Use the cardboard model to show what happens when you launch a "marble rocket" upward, away from the earth's surface. Use what you know about scientific methods to find out.

1.2 *The Force of Gravity*

► *Why does the moon orbit Earth?*

In the year 1665, a young man named Isaac Newton asked a simple question: Why does the moon orbit Earth? Newton knew that the moon goes around and around Earth. But he couldn't explain why. All year long Newton kept asking why the moon orbits Earth. He finally discovered the answer right under his feet.

Newton discovered the answer to his question by thinking about apples. He wondered why ripe apples fall down from apple trees. There must be a force that pulls the apples down to Earth, he thought. And if a force pulls the apples down to Earth, maybe a force also pulls the moon around and around Earth. Are those two forces the same, or are they different?

Newton kept thinking about apples, orbits, and forces. At last he came up with the answer. The two forces are the same! The force that pulls apples to the ground is the same as the force that pulls the moon around Earth. That force is called gravity. In this lesson, you will find out how gravity works. But first you will read about systems.

Systems in Space

Systems are all around you. For example, a rider and a bicycle form a system. The rider starts the bicycle by turning the pedals. The pedals turn the chain; the chain turns the gears; the gears turn the wheels. All those parts work together. As long as the rider keeps pedaling, the system keeps working.

A system you know quite well is your body. Blood carries oxygen and nutrients to your cells. Cells release energy so muscles, like your heart, can do their work. As long as these parts work together, you stay active and healthy.

The sun and Earth always work together. Year after year Earth orbits the sun. Year after year the sun shines on Earth. Because they work together, the sun and Earth can be called a **system**—a set of parts that affect each other.

The moon and Earth are also very different from one another. And they too form a system. Notice in the picture how the Earth and moon system is similar to the sun and Earth system. The moon is smaller than Earth, and it orbits Earth. Month after month the moon keeps orbiting Earth, even as Earth is orbiting the sun. Why does the moon orbit Earth? Why does Earth orbit the sun? The answer to both of those questions is gravity.

▲ The sun and Earth form a system, and Earth and the moon form another system.

How Gravity Behaves

You can't see gravity, and you can't touch it, but gravity is always present. **Gravity** (grav′ ə tē) is a force of attraction between objects. An apple and Earth are both objects. Gravity pulls them together. Because of gravity, the apple falls to Earth.

The force of gravity between two objects depends on how far apart those objects are. An apple grows on a branch just a few meters above Earth. Because the apple and Earth are so close together, the force of gravity between them is strong. But if the apple were 150 million kilometers from Earth, the force of gravity between them would be weak. The greater the distance between two objects, the weaker the force of gravity is between them.

Gravity is not only affected by the distance between objects. Gravity is also affected by mass. What is **mass**? It's the amount of matter an object contains. Earth has much more matter than an apple, so Earth has much more mass than an apple. Likewise, the sun has more matter than Earth, so the sun has much more mass than Earth.

The more mass two objects have, the greater the force of gravity is between them. Taken together, the sun and Earth have much more mass than the apple and Earth. So even though the sun is 150 million kilometers from Earth, the force of gravity between the sun and Earth is strong, because of their large combined mass. But if the apple were 150 million kilometers from Earth, the force of gravity between the apple and Earth would be weak. Not only would the apple and Earth be far apart, but their combined mass would be small.

Effects of Gravity

Moon

Path with no gravity

Moon Path with gravity

▲ The moon orbits Earth because of the pull of gravity between them.

Gravity and Orbits

Gravity pulls Earth and the moon together. But the moon doesn't fall to Earth like an apple. In the picture on page 12 you can see that the moon is always moving. What if the moon wasn't pulled by Earth's gravity? Then it would move in a straight path away from Earth. Notice in the picture that gravity pulls the moon out of its straight path. Because of the pull of gravity, the moon keeps falling in a path that curves around Earth. That curved path is the moon's orbit.

But why doesn't Earth orbit the moon? Because when two objects attract each other, the object with less mass will move more easily. The moon has much less mass than Earth. Therefore, the moon orbits around Earth instead of Earth orbiting around the moon.

By using what you have learned about gravity and mass, you can explain why an apple falls to Earth. To begin with, the force of gravity between the apple and Earth is strong because they are so close together. And because the apple has less mass than Earth, it moves more easily than Earth. Therefore the apple always falls to Earth.

Checkpoint

1. What is a system?
2. What happens to the force of gravity between two objects that are moving farther apart?
3. What path would the moon take if it weren't pulled by Earth's gravity?
4. **Take Action!** Select two objects. Show how you can decrease the pull of gravity between them. Also show which one would revolve around the other if they were in space.

Activity

The Path of Light

Instruments like binoculars and periscopes work because of the way light travels. Try this activity to find out how light travels.

Picture A

Picture B

Picture C

Gather These Materials

3 file cards
hole punch
clay

black construction paper
flashlight

Follow This Procedure

1 Make a chart like the one on the next page. Record your observations in your chart.

2 Place 3 file cards on top of each other so the corners are lined up. Punch a hole in the center of all 3 cards at once.

3 Place a lump of clay at the bottom of each card to hold the cards upright.

4 Place the 3 file cards with their holes lined up. They should be about 5 cm apart. (Picture A)

5 Hold the black construction paper in back of the last file card. (Picture B)

Predict: **Will light be able to travel through the cards onto the black paper?**

6 Turn on the flashlight. Shine the flashlight through the hole in the first card. Observe what happens to the light and record the results in the chart.

Record Your Results

Position of holes	Observations
When holes are lined up	
When holes aren't lined up	

Predict: *What would happen to the light if the holes were not lined up?*

7 Move the middle card so that the holes no longer line up. (Picture C)

8 Shine the flashlight through the holes again. What happens? Record your observations on your chart.

State Your Conclusions

1. Describe how light travels.
2. Why can't you see around corners?

Let's Experiment

Now that you've seen how light travels, can you use mirrors to direct light around corners? Use what you know about scientific methods to find out.

1.3 *Light and Shadows*

▼ *In a partial eclipse the moon moves between Earth and the sun. This blocks most of the sun's light from reaching Earth.*

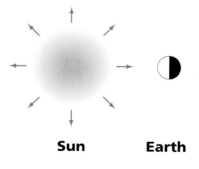

▼ *Sunlight travels away from the sun in straight line paths.*

Sun   Earth

➤ *Half of Earth is always in darkness while the other half is always in light.*

How can the moon cover the sun?

In Baja California, Mexico, the morning of July 11, 1991, began like any other. The sun came up in the east and slowly rose in the sky. Not long after sunrise, however, something unusual happened. A large, dark object started to creep across the sun.

Over the next hour and a half the object covered more and more of the sun. The sky turned darker. Finally, at 10:24 A.M., day seemed to turn into night.

During the next five minutes, the morning of July 11 was like the night before. Then the object that blocked the sun began to move away. One and a half hours later the sun shone as brightly as ever.

Did a giant cloud block the sun? The object was giant, but it wasn't a cloud. It was the moon. In this lesson, you will learn how the moon's movement can keep the sun's light from reaching Earth. You will also learn about how Earth's movements cause day and night.

Catching the Rays

A baseball can help you understand day and night on Earth. When you look at a baseball you can see only half of it. The other half faces away from you. No matter how fast you spin the baseball, you can see only one half at a time. In the same way, one half of Earth is always facing the sun. The other half is always facing away from the sun. That side is dark because no sunlight can reach it. As Earth rotates, one part is always spinning into darkness. Another part of Earth, on the other side, is always spinning into sunlight.

Notice in the picture on page 16 that sunlight travels in rays that move away from the sun. Light moves incredibly fast—faster than any other speed we know. In just over eight short minutes, light can zoom across the 150 million kilometers of dark space that separates the sun and Earth. The sun's rays don't light up this space. They light up only Earth, the moon, and other solid objects that they hit. The rays can't pass through these solid objects. Therefore, as Earth rotates, the half facing the sun is light. The other half of Earth is dark, as shown in the picture below.

Traveling Time

Sunlight has a long way to go to reach the planets in our solar system. Each planet is a different distance from the sun, so sunlight reaches each one at a different time.

The graphs show how far sunlight travels in minutes and hours.

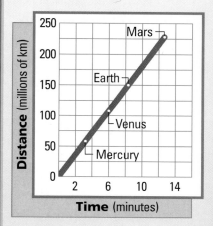

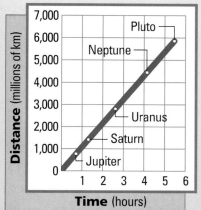

What Did You Find Out?
1. *How many kilometers away from the sun is Mercury? Pluto?*
2. *How long does sunlight take to reach Mercury? Pluto?*

Moonlight: Reflections on Sections

As the moon orbits Earth, it seems to change shape.

The moon, our closest neighbor in space, is shaped like a ball. Yet from day to day, its shape seems to change. Sometimes the moon appears as a round circle. At other times only thin slivers can be seen.

These changes are called phases of the moon. The phases appear in a pattern that repeats every $29\frac{1}{3}$ days. This period is the time the moon takes to orbit Earth.

But the moon only seems to change shape. The shape of the moon that we see depends on how much of the sunlit half of the moon is facing Earth. And that depends on the position of the moon in its orbit around Earth.

1 New Moon Moon is between Earth and sun; sunlit side of moon faces away.

3 First Quarter One week later, half the moon's sunlit side faces Earth.

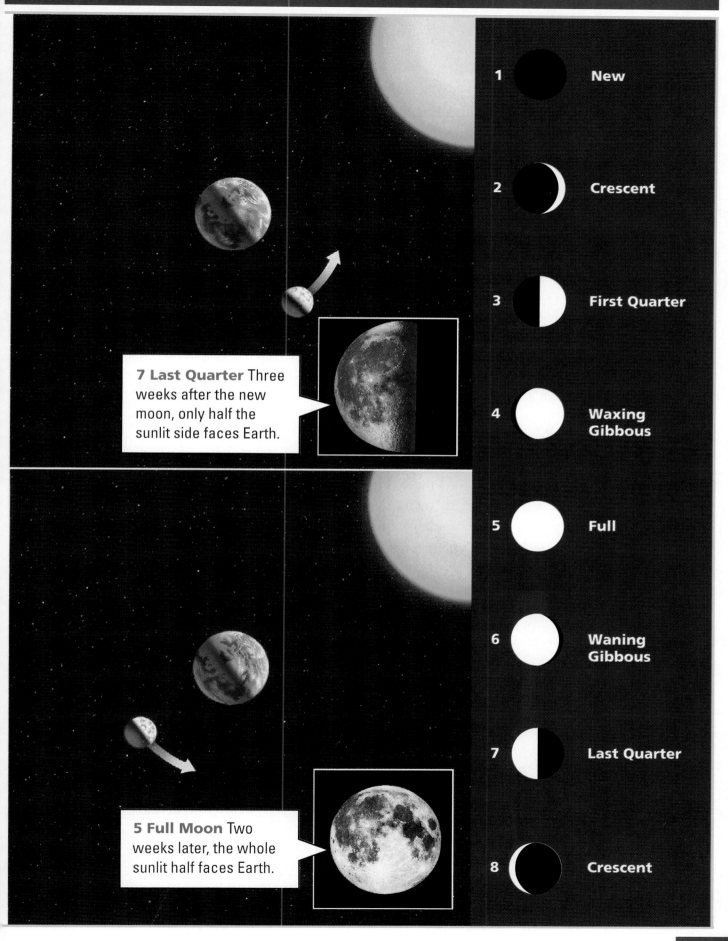

7 Last Quarter Three weeks after the new moon, only half the sunlit side faces Earth.

5 Full Moon Two weeks later, the whole sunlit half faces Earth.

1   New

2   Crescent

3   First Quarter

4   Waxing Gibbous

5   Full

6   Waning Gibbous

7   Last Quarter

8   Crescent

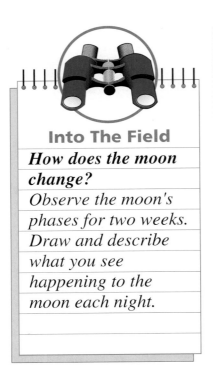

Into The Field

How does the moon change?

Observe the moon's phases for two weeks. Draw and describe what you see happening to the moon each night.

▼ The sun's light is blocked by the moon in a solar eclipse.

Making a Shadow

When the moon moves directly between the sun and Earth so that all three are lined up in a straight line, a **solar eclipse** (sō′ lər i klips′) begins. During a solar eclipse, the moon blocks sunlight from reaching Earth, making a shadow of the moon on Earth.

Find the moon's shadow on Earth in the picture below. The center of the moon's shadow is dark. Anyone in this part of the shadow sees a total solar eclipse. The moon totally blocks the sun. Only a bright ring around the sun can be seen. When the moon blocks only part of the sun from your view, you see a partial solar eclipse. The people in the outer rim of the moon's shadow see a partial solar eclipse. The moon moves quickly, so a total solar eclipse is brief. It can last anywhere from a few seconds to seven and a half minutes. An example of a total and of a partial solar eclipse is shown on the next page. On July 11, 1991, people in Baja California, Mexico, saw a total solar eclipse. At the same time, people in most of the other parts of North America saw a partial solar eclipse.

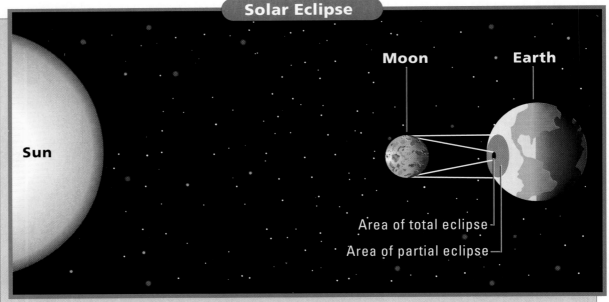

Solar Eclipse

Sun

Moon

Earth

Area of total eclipse

Area of partial eclipse

◀ *During a total solar eclipse, the sun is completely blocked from view on Earth. During a partial solar eclipse, only part of the sun is blocked from view.*

Notice in the diagram at the right that sometimes Earth passes between the sun and the moon. When that happens, Earth casts a shadow on the moon. That's called a lunar eclipse. Lunar eclipses are more common than solar eclipses.

Joining the System

In the last lesson, you learned that the sun and Earth form a system. You also learned that Earth and the moon form a system. Both of those systems combined form a larger system. It is made up of the sun, Earth, and the moon. This system is part of a still larger system. It is called the solar system. You'll learn more about the solar system in the next chapter.

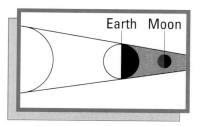

▲ *When Earth moves directly between the moon and the sun, a lunar eclipse occurs.*

Checkpoint

1. Why is Earth always half dark?
2. What determines how much of the moon is visible to us here on Earth?
3. How are Earth, the sun, and the moon lined up during a solar eclipse?
4. Name four systems to which Earth belongs.
5. Take Action! Make a calendar that shows the phases of the moon each night for a month. Try to predict the phases that will occur next.

Inferring

When you use the information you have to make a guess about what is likely to be true, you are inferring. Scientists often make inferences. They may need to study something too far away in time or space to observe directly. Scientists might make inferences based on the data they gather. Or they might use what they already know about a similar event to infer facts.

Thinking It Through

What causes an eclipse of the moon? Use these questions to help you find out.

What do I know for sure about an eclipse of the moon?

I know that in an eclipse of the moon, the moon becomes dark at a time when it would usually shine. I also know that the moon shines by reflecting sunlight.

What event do I know that is like an eclipse of the moon?

I know about an eclipse of the sun.

What information about a solar eclipse helps explain an eclipse of the moon?

The moon causes a solar eclipse when it passes between the earth and the sun, casting a shadow on the earth's surface.

Can I make an inference?

Maybe something casts a shadow during an eclipse of the moon. But what makes the shadow? Maybe the earth comes between the sun and the moon and casts a shadow on the moon.

When you need to make an inference, keep these steps in mind:

1. Figure out what you know for sure.

2. Think of a similar event.

3. What do you know about the similar event that could fill in a gap in your information about this event?

4. Make an inference based on the similar event.

Your Turn

Imagine you are living on the moon. Would you be able to see an eclipse of the sun there? Use data from the chapter to help you find a likely answer.

Chapter Review

Thinking Back

1. Explain the difference between a **revolution** and a **rotation** of Earth.
2. What is **gravity** and how does it affect a system?
3. Explain why **mass** causes Earth to revolve around the sun rather than the sun around Earth.
4. Name a **system** and explain why it is a system.
5. When does a **solar eclipse** occur?
6. A planet has two moons of equal mass, one at a distance of 100,000 kilometers and another at 1,000,000 kilometers. Which moon would have a stronger force of gravity between it and the planet? Why?
7. Explain why half of Earth is always dark.
8. Describe the changes the moon goes through as it orbits Earth once.

Connecting Ideas

1. Copy the concept map. Use the terms at the right to complete the map about revolving.

moon   sun

A. _____ *revolves around* B. **Earth** *revolves around* C. _____

2. Write a sentence or two about the ideas shown in the concept map.

Gathering Evidence

1. In the Activity on page 8, how did you know where the force of gravity was the greatest and the slightest?
2. In the Activity on page 14, how did you know the shape of the path of light?

Doing Science!

1. *Create an activity* that would show how an object with less mass is more easily pulled by gravity than one with more mass.
2. *Design an activity* that would show the phases of the moon.

The Solar System

Our car is like this in the summer. You can't even sit in the seats.

How can you trap heat?

Think about containers in your room that light can pass through. Which one traps the most heat from the sun? To find out, place a thermometer inside the empty container. Then, place the container in the sun. Put another thermometer outside the container. After 30 minutes, read each thermometer.

For Discussion

1. What happens to the temperature inside your container?

2. How could you make it trap more heat?

2.1 *The Inner Planets*

What is it like on other planets?

It's a good thing that Earth is part of the solar system. Without the pull of gravity between the sun and Earth, Earth would find itself traveling off into space. Without the sun's light and energy, Earth would be a very cold and dark world. However, Earth does orbit the sun and so it has a place in the solar system. But Earth is not the only planet that is affected by the sun's energy and gravity.

People have always wondered what it's like on other bodies in the solar system. The moon is the only place people have been able to visit in person to answer that question. On July 20, 1969, astronaut Neil Armstrong was the first human to set foot on the moon. Six other missions visited the moon after that to explore, collect samples, and conduct experiments. Space probes sent from Earth without crews have been able to travel vast distances through the solar system. The probes have found that the planets in the solar system are very different from one another.

Find Mercury, Venus, Earth, and Mars on the map. They are the inner planets because they orbit closest to the sun. The outer planets—Jupiter, Saturn, Uranus, Neptune, and Pluto—orbit much farther away. In this lesson, you will learn how being in the solar system affects the inner planets.

Pluto
Neptune
Mercury
Venus
Earth
Jupiter
Mars
Saturn
Uranus

▲ *The solar system*

The sun

The Sun—The Shining Sphere

The sun is the largest, brightest, and hottest object in the solar system. It is also the center of the solar system. The sun has more mass than all the other objects in our solar system put together. As a result, gravitational force causes all the planets to orbit around the sun—even planets as distant as Neptune and Pluto.

The powerful sun is mostly made of a gas called hydrogen. In turn, the hydrogen is made of tiny particles called atoms. At the sun's center, hydrogen atoms may reach temperatures as high as 15 million degrees Celsius (°C). The higher the temperature, the faster the atoms move. Some of the atoms move so fast that they smash into each other and form a gas called helium. And when the hydrogen atoms change into helium, they also release energy. The energy heats up the sun and makes it shine. The sun has enough hydrogen to stay hot and shining for about 4 billion years.

Mercury—The Hot and Cold Planet

The closest planet to the sun is Mercury. Because it is so close to the sun, it is difficult to study Mercury from Earth. The brightness of the sun makes it hard to see. Spacecraft flying past Mercury have sent back to Earth pictures and information about this planet.

In some ways, Mercury is similar to our moon. This small planet is only a little larger than our moon and, like the moon, it is covered by dust, rocks, and bowl-shaped holes called craters. Thousands of **meteorites** (mē′tē ə rīts′)—chunks of rock from outer space—formed the craters by crashing into Mercury. You can see Mercury's rocky surface and some of its many craters in the picture shown below.

Mercury

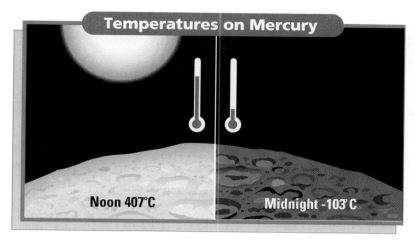

Temperatures on Mercury

Noon 407°C   Midnight -103°C

When Mercury has rotated once around its axis, 59 Earth days have gone by. Long days combined with closeness to the sun and a very thin atmosphere explain how Mercury can be so hot and so cold. During the day, Mercury's thin atmosphere can't protect the planet from the sun's heating rays. The diagram above shows that noontime temperatures on Mercury can reach 407°C. Afternoons can sizzle to 427°C. At night, the atmosphere can't keep the heat in, so the temperature can drop to about −183°C.

Venus—Cloudy Neighbor

Venus has a very thick atmosphere. The picture shows the thick, swirling clouds of carbon dioxide and acid that surround Venus. Powerful winds that move at speeds of over 300 kilometers per hour keep the clouds moving at all times. The atmosphere presses down on Venus like a very heavy blanket. In 1975, two large space probes from Earth landed on Venus. The probes lasted less than two hours before they were flattened by Venus's crushing atmosphere and damaged by the heat.

It takes Venus a little longer to rotate once around its axis than to revolve once around the sun. So, on Venus, a day is slightly longer than a year.

▼ *Venus*

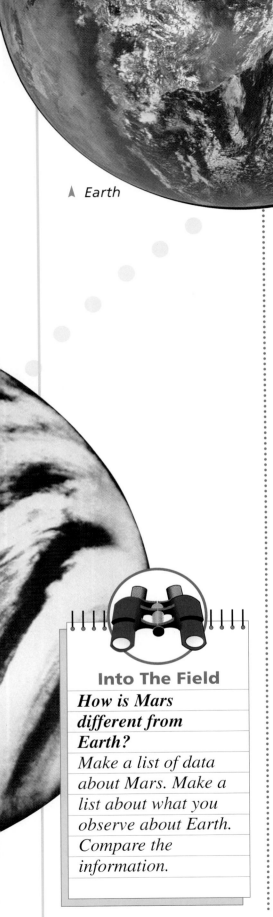

Earth

Compare the pictures of Venus and Earth. Venus is about the same size as Earth. Like Earth, Venus has mountains, valleys, and plains. It even has a volcano bigger than any mountain on Earth. But Venus has no water. In the Discover Activity, you saw how heat can be trapped inside a container. The heat on Venus is unbearable—about 450°C, enough to melt some kinds of metal! The thick atmosphere on Venus traps the sun's energy and holds it close to the surface, day and night. Venus is hotter than Mercury, even though Mercury is closer to the sun. Life as we know it could not survive on Venus. Only rocks can exist in Venus's high temperatures and the crushing pressure of its atmosphere.

Mars—the Red Planet

Mars is a little bit like Mercury, a little bit like Venus, and a lot like Earth. As you can see in the picture on page 29, Mars looks reddish. Mars is about half as wide as the Earth.

As on Mercury, craters dot the surface of Mars. The nights are much colder than the days. As on Venus, the atmosphere of Mars is mostly carbon dioxide. But Mars's atmosphere is not thick enough to trap the sun's heat.

Like Earth, Mars has changing seasons, and days that are about 25 hours long. The average winter temperature on Mars is a chilly –125°C. Summer temperatures can sometimes get as high as 0°C. Mars also has north and south poles. The poles are covered with caps of frozen carbon dioxide, called dry ice. When the poles heat up, the ice caps melt and get smaller. When the poles cool down, the ice caps get larger.

Into The Field

How is Mars different from Earth?

Make a list of data about Mars. Make a list about what you observe about Earth. Compare the information.

Some of the ice at the poles may also be frozen water. Mars might have had a lot of water millions of years ago. The many valleys and canyons on the surface of Mars could have been formed by rushing rivers. The flat areas could be the bottoms of lakes that dried up long ago. However, the surface is now dry and the air contains only traces of water vapor. Notice in the picture below that the surface of Mars is dry, reddish, and dusty. The redness comes from rusted iron in the rocks.

Mars appears to be lifeless now. But does that mean there never was any life on Mars? In the summer of 1976, two space probes from Earth landed on the surface of Mars. The probes studied the air and the soil. They took pictures and sent the information back to Earth. Scientists found no signs of life after studying the information. Even so, some scientists think Mars could support life. Perhaps someday astronauts will go to Mars to try to answer this mysterious question.

▼ *Mars*

▲ *The surface of Mars is dry, dusty, and reddish.*

Checkpoint

1. In what ways does the sun affect the rest of the solar system?
2. How did Mercury get so many craters on its surface?
3. What causes Venus to be hotter than Mercury?
4. What causes Mars to be so cold?
5. **Take Action!** Use marbles, tennis balls, and golf balls to show how the inner planets compare in size.

Activity

What Affects the Temperature of a Planet?

Many planets in our solar system are very hot or cold. Try this activity to learn more about how the sun heats the planets.

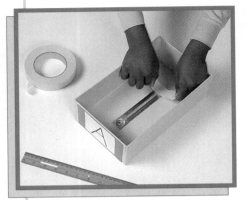

Picture A

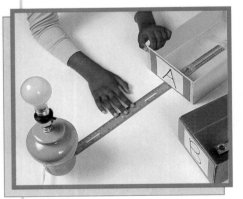

Picture B

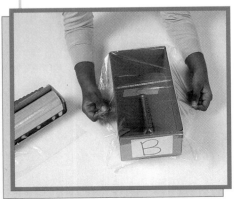

Picture C

Gather These Materials

2 shoe boxes
marker
2 thermometers
tape

metric ruler
lamp
plastic wrap

Follow This Procedure

Part A

1. Make a chart like the one on the next page. Record your observations in your chart.

2. Use a marker to label two shoe boxes, A and B. Each shoe box will represent a different planet.

3. Tape a thermometer to the inside bottom of each box. (Picture A) Read and record the starting temperature in each box.

4. Using the metric ruler, place Box A 30 cm away from the light bulb in the lamp. The light bulb will represent the sun. Place Box B 60 cm from the light bulb. (Picture B)

Predict: *In which shoe box will the air heat up faster?*

5. Measure the temperature inside each box after 10 minutes. Continue taking temperatures and recording every 10 minutes for half an hour.

Part B

1 Make a copy of the chart you made in Part A.

2 Shut off the lamp and begin this part after both thermometers return to room temperature. Place Boxes A and B 30 cm from the lamp.

3 Cover the opening of one box with plastic wrap. (Picture C)

4 Measure and record the temperature inside each box every 10 minutes for half an hour.

Record Your Results

Temperature	Box	
	A	B
At start		
10 minutes		
20 minutes		
30 minutes		

State Your Conclusions

1. In part A, which box was warmer after half an hour? Explain what happened.

2. Use what you learned in Part A to explain how distance from the sun affects the temperature of each planet.

3. In Part B, which box was warmer after half an hour? Explain what happened.

4. Using what you learned in Part B, explain how the plastic wrap acted like an atmosphere.

Let's Experiment

Now that you have learned how planets heat up, design an experiment to explain why the temperatures on Venus can be hotter than on Mercury. Use what you know about scientific methods to find out.

2.2 *The Outer Planets*

What are the outer planets?

Gaze at a clear night sky for just a few minutes. You'll probably see a meteor—sometimes called a falling star. Meteors aren't really stars. But they're as bright as stars and they really are falling. **Meteors** (mē′tē ərz) are chunks of rock that burn up brightly as they fall through Earth's atmosphere. Luckily for us, most meteors burn up before they reach Earth's surface. Those that do reach the surface are called meteorites.

Some meteors come from the asteroid belt—a large group of rocks that orbits the sun just beyond the inner planets. Asteroids come in all shapes and sizes. The largest one is about as wide as the state of Texas. The smallest might be smaller than a basketball.

Asteroids often smash into each other. When that happens they crumble into pieces of rock that fly in all directions. Many head toward the sun. A few of these become Earth's meteors. Others speed toward the outer planets of the solar system: Jupiter, Saturn, Uranus, Neptune, and Pluto.

➤ *Jupiter*

Planets of Gas

The pictures on these pages show Jupiter and Saturn, the largest planets in the solar system. Each one is about ten times wider than Earth. Unlike the inner planets, Jupiter and Saturn are mostly made of layers of liquid hydrogen and helium, but they probably have solid cores. Thick, swirling, colorful clouds of gas surround both planets. The Great Red Spot of Jupiter has long been visible among its clouds of gas.

Unlike the inner planets, Jupiter and Saturn create more heat than they receive from the sun. Their centers may be as hot as 24,000°C. That's hot! But it's not hot enough to heat the clouds that surround both planets. Near the tops of the clouds on both Jupiter and Saturn the temperature is about −150°C. That's cold! Rings of dust and ice spin around the equators of these two giant planets. Jupiter's rings are so dark and thin they're almost invisible. Saturn's rings were first seen in the 1600s. But telescopes weren't very powerful then, so people thought there was only one ring. Since then seven major rings have been found. Notice in the picture that Saturn's rings appear as many colorful, bright bands.

Dozens of moons orbit above, below, and beyond the rings of each planet. Jupiter has at least 16 moons, Saturn has at least 24 moons. The moons are as different from each other as fire and ice. Io, a moon of Jupiter, has active volcanoes. Europa, another of Jupiter's moons, has a vast frozen plain of water. Titan, one of Saturn's moons, is larger than Mercury. Its atmosphere is thought to be similar to Earth's atmosphere when Earth was very young.

▲ Saturn has hundreds of thin rings made up of ice particles. The color in these rings was added by a computer. To your eye the rings would appear white.

New Worlds

You're about to visit the planets. But what will you bring?

Mercury The closest to the sun, Mercury is very hot during the day. It has little atmosphere.

Venus Earth's nearest neighbor, Venus has an atmosphere that is mostly carbon dioxide, and its thick clouds are made of acid.

Earth You explore this planet every day.

Mars Its red surface is similar to Earth's, but much colder. Any water is frozen all year long.

Jupiter The largest of all the planets, Jupiter is made mostly of gases and liquids.

Saturn Almost as large as Jupiter, Saturn is famous for its rings.

Uranus and **Neptune** Both are blue-green, very cold, and very far from the sun.

Pluto The smallest and farthest from the sun, Pluto takes 248 years to circle the sun.

Something cool would be nice on Mercury. But in this heat, it would evaporate right away.

Use at night on any planet. The clouds on Venus are so thick, you might need a flashlight all the time.

The very, very bright sunlight on Mercury would make it impossible to see without eye protection.

Think about it: if you're 12 years old on Earth, you'd be 48 on Mercury, 6 on Mars, and 1 year old on Jupiter.

Mercury has craters. Mars has extinct volcanoes. But for now, climbing mountains on Earth will do.

Distant Planets

Uranus and Neptune are smaller versions of Jupiter and Saturn. Like their larger neighbors, Uranus and Neptune probably have solid inner cores surrounded by layers of liquid and gas. They also have incredibly varied moons. One of these moons appears to have volcanoes that could have erupted water and ice.

Notice in the picture that Uranus and Neptune are nearly the same size and color. Both planets are about four times wider than Earth. Both are bluish in color and both have thin, wispy rings. Even though Neptune is much farther from the sun than Uranus, both planets have about the same surface temperature: an icy −215° C.

Cloudy Edges

The small picture below shows Pluto, the farthest known planet from the sun. Pluto is the only planet that a space probe hasn't studied, or flown by, so we know very little about it. We do know that Pluto has one moon.

▼ *Uranus*

➤ *Neptune, and Pluto on the far right.*

We also know that Pluto is the smallest planet—even tinier than Earth's moon. Unlike the other outer planets, Pluto is made of rock and ice.

Pluto's orbit differs from the orbits of all the other planets. Between 1979 and 1999 Pluto's orbit brings it closer than Neptune to the sun. It takes Pluto 248 Earth years to complete its long journey around the sun. Temperatures on Pluto are just a few degrees colder than those found on Uranus and Neptune. If you could stand on Pluto, the sun would look just like any other star: a distant point of light.

Does Pluto mark the edge of the solar system? Probably not. Billions and billions of kilometers from Pluto there may be a vast cloud of comets. Comets are icy balls of frozen gas and dust. The cloud of comets is called the Oort Cloud. The Oort Cloud may surround the entire solar system. It could contain more than a trillion comets orbiting the sun. Some comets disappear, never to be seen again. Others continually orbit the sun. Halley's comet, last seen in 1986, will return 76 years later, in 2062.

The comets that we sometimes see streaking through the night sky may come from the Oort Cloud. They are far different from the warm, comfortable planet we call Earth.

Checkpoint

1. How are Jupiter and Saturn similar to the sun?
2. Which group of planets has more in common, the inner or the outer planets?
3. List several ways that Uranus and Neptune are alike.
4. Where do most comets come from?
5. **Take Action!** Make a chart that compares the five outer planets. Compare how they are the same or different.

INVESTIGATE

Planet Names

Are the day names related to the names of objects in the solar system? Let's investigate.

What To Do
A. Copy the two charts below; make each one long enough to fit all seven days of the week.
B. Fill in the English chart; start with Sunday.
C. Fill in the Spanish chart using an English-Spanish dictionary.
D. In the Sky Body column, match these sky bodies with the English or Spanish name that sounds most similar: Mars, Saturn, Venus, Sun, Mercury, Moon, Jupiter.

Day of the Week		Sky Body Name
English	Sunday	
Spanish	domingo	

What Did You Find Out?
1. *Are the names of the days related to the names of objects in the solar system? Explain.*
2. *Write a myth about how Sunday got its name.*

Activity

How Can You Make a Model of the Solar System?

A scale model is a small version of the real thing. In this activity, you can make a scale model of the solar system.

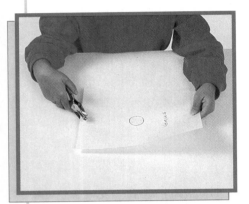

Picture A

Picture B

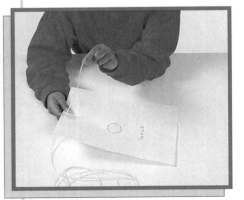

Picture C

Gather These Materials

art paper
colored markers
metric ruler
hole punch

masking tape
meter sticks
ball of string

Follow This Procedure

Team 1

1. Members of Team 1 should draw and label each of the nine planets on a separate piece of paper. Draw in some features of each planet. Use the chart on the next page to find the diameter of each planet in this scale model. Use a metric ruler to draw each planet with its correct diameter.

2. Use a hole punch to make a hole at the top of each drawing. Put masking tape above and below the hole to reinforce it. (Picture A)

Team 2

1. Use the chart to find the distance from the sun to each planet. Your teacher will tell you where the sun will be in your scale model. Using that location as the starting point, measure the distance to each planet using a meter stick.

Predict: Which planets will be visible from the earth's position?

Planet	Diameter Scale: 1 cm = 2,000 km	Distance from the sun Scale: 1 m = 150 million km
Mercury	3.4 cm	0.38 m
Venus	6.2 cm	0.72 m
Earth	6.4 cm	1 m
Mars	3.4 cm	1.5 m
Jupiter	71 cm	5.2 m
Saturn	60 cm	9.5 m
Uranus	26 cm	19 m
Neptune	22.4 cm	30 m
Pluto	1.2 cm	39 m

2 Write out each planet name on a piece of masking tape. Place each label on the floor at its correct distance from the sun. (Picture B)

3 Thread the pictures of the nine planets in order on a piece of string. Nine students, each holding a drawing, should take a "space walk" along the string to its label on the floor. (Picture C)

State Your Conclusions

1. Are you surprised by the sizes or distances of the planets? Explain.

2. In your model of the solar system you have used one scale for the planets' size and another for their distance from the sun. Why do you think this was done?

3. Most of the solar system is space. Why do you agree or disagree with this statement?

Let's Experiment

Now that you have learned about scale models, why do you think some planets were not discovered for a long time? Use what you know about scientific methods to find out.

Ordering Planets

Suppose you found the index of this book on the first page and part of the first lesson on the last page. Imagine how hard it would be to read and understand.

Scientists organize facts into a certain order for the same reason a book is ordered in a certain way. Ordering facts makes them easier to understand.

Thinking It Through

How you order things depends on what you need to know about them. For example, suppose you wanted to know which planets take longer to orbit the sun. It would make sense to order the planets according to their distances from the sun.

Suppose instead you wanted to know whether Earth is a large planet, a small one, or somewhere in between. In that case, you would want to order the planets according to their size.

You can order things by finding the greatest number. For instance, look for the planet that is the greatest number of kilometers from the sun, or the planet that is the largest size. Then find the next greatest number, and so on until everything is in order.

Order may be shown by making a list, a table, or a drawing. In the drawing below the planets are shown according to their sizes. Note that you can easily tell which is the largest planet and which is the smallest. This way of ordering helps show how large Earth is compared to the other planets. Can you think of one other fact this order helps to show?

Your Turn

Choose a new way to order the planets. Order the planets according to your way. Explain why you chose this particular order.

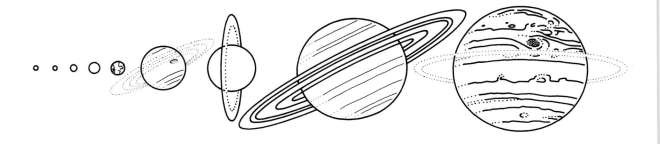

Chapter Review

Thinking Back

1. What have **meteorites** done to the surface of Mercury?

2. How is Venus different from Mercury?

3. Why is Venus not a good place for humans to live?

4. How is Mars different from Earth?

5. What is a **meteor**?

6. What causes the rings around the equators of Jupiter and Saturn?

7. Which two planets are closer to the sun than Earth is?

8. In what ways are Uranus and Neptune similar to the two giant planets?

9. In what ways is Pluto different from the other outer planets?

Connecting Ideas

1. Copy the concept map. Use the terms at the right to complete the map about the planets.

Earth	Mars	Neptune
Pluto	Uranus	Saturn
	Venus	

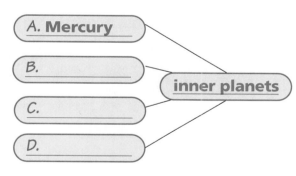

A. **Mercury**

B. _____

C. _____

D. _____

inner planets

outer planets

E. **Jupiter**

F. _____

G. _____

H. _____

I. _____

2. Write a sentence or two about the ideas shown in the concept map.

Gathering Evidence

1. In the Activity on page 30, how did you conclude how the sun heats the planets?

2. In the Activity on page 38, how did you conclude that the solar system is mostly space?

Doing Science!

1. **Choose one planet** and make up an animal that could survive there.

2. **Choose one planet** and write a skit about a journey to that planet.

3

The Blue Planet

Discover Activity

Is there water in soil?

Take a clump of soil and feel it with your hands. Do you think it contains water? Can you see the water? Can you smell it? Find a way to collect any water that the soil might contain.

It's sticking to my hand so it must be wet!

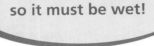

Wear cover goggles for this activity.

For Discussion

1. How did you show that soil contains water?

2. How can you show that water is in the air?

3.1 System of the Spheres

Why do astronauts wear spacesuits?

On July 20, 1969, astronauts Neil Armstrong and Edwin Aldrin became the first people ever to walk upon the dry and airless surface of the moon. In order to breathe, the astronauts had to wear bulky spacesuits that provided them with air. The spacesuits also protected them from extreme temperatures, harmful solar rays, and even tiny meteorites. Without their suits, the astronauts would have died instantly.

Looking up into space they could see the planet we call Earth. How inviting Earth must have looked to them! They could see enormous blue oceans shimmering beneath the fluffy white clouds in Earth's atmosphere. They could also see solid masses of land.

Unlike the moon and other planets, Earth has air that you can breathe and water that you can drink. It has soil in which plants can grow. Earth has all the ingredients necessary to support life as we know it. On Earth you don't need to wear a spacesuit.

▼ *Part of Earth as seen from space*

Our Planet's Spheres

Earth's three spheres provide all that living things need.

The **atmosphere** is Earth's outer covering of air. It provides the gases that plants and animals need to survive. It protects living things from being damaged by too much sunlight.

The **hydrosphere** (hī′ drə sfir) provides living things with water. Oceans, lakes, rivers, and streams are all part of the hydrosphere. Earth alone has water in its liquid state available in such great abundance. In fact, water covers almost three quarters of Earth's surface.

The **lithosphere** (lith′ ə sfir) is Earth's solid, rocky outer shell. It contains soil, rocks, and minerals that are needed for plants. And, plants provide the food that animals need.

The Interactive Spheres

The picture below shows the interactions of Earth's atmosphere, hydrosphere, and lithosphere. While each sphere is quite different from the others, parts of each sphere can be found in the other spheres. For example, the atmosphere contains drops of water from the hydrosphere and bits of dust from the lithosphere. Solids and gases mix in the oceans and lakes of the hydrosphere. You found out in the Discover Activity that even the ground beneath your feet—part of the lithosphere—can hold water.

The three spheres together form a system in which each sphere affects the others. How can they form a system? The answer begins with the sun! Because of the sun's energy, different parts of the spheres are able to move from one sphere to another. For example, the water of the hydrosphere travels constantly between ocean, air, and land. The journey begins when the sun's energy heats the ocean, causing water to evaporate.

▼ The hydrosphere, atmosphere, and lithosphere are in close contact.

Rising water vapor can cool and change back into tiny droplets of liquid. These droplets form clouds that move with the air across the ocean and over the ground of the lithosphere. Rain pours down on the land in mighty storms. The water carries dirt and rocks into rushing streams.

The streams flow together into large rivers, which empty into the oceans. Soon the water will evaporate again. It will continue its never-ending journey through the atmosphere, the lithosphere, and the hydrosphere.

The Sphere of Life

The interaction of the atmosphere, the lithosphere, and the hydrosphere creates another sphere—the sphere of life. No other planet that we know of in the solar system contains life. The system of the spheres makes life possible on Earth.

Life thrives in each of the three spheres. Living things need air, water, and nutrients, found in each sphere. Living things are found in the lower atmosphere and upper lithosphere. Life is found all through the hydrosphere—even to the darkest depths of the oceans. The sphere of life is called the **biosphere** (bī′ə sfir).Within it live fish of the ocean, birds of the air, trees of the forest, and you.

Checkpoint

1. What important things can be found in each of the three spheres that enables living things to survive?
2. What allows parts of one sphere to move into another?
3. Where is the biosphere found on Earth?
4. Take Action! Pour water into a container of soil. Notice the air bubbles on the soil's surface. Where does the air come from?

Activity

Is There Life in All Three Spheres?

Living things can be found in the strangest places. Try this activity to find out where the living things are near you.

Picture A

Picture B

Gather These Materials

paper cup
spoon
soil
white paper towel
hand lens
reference books

pond water
petri dish
medicine dropper
depression slide
microscope

Follow This Procedure

Part A

1 Make a chart like the one on the next page. Record your observations in your chart.

2 Use a paper cup and spoon to collect some moist soil. Your teacher will tell you where to look.

> **Predict:** *What kinds of living things are you likely to see in the soil?*

3 Empty the soil sample onto a white paper towel. (Picture A)

4 Use a hand lens to look at the living things that you see in the soil. (Picture B) You may need a book to help identify the living things. List their names on the chart. Draw pictures of the living things that you find.

5 Wash your hands when you have finished.

Picture C

Part B

1 Get a sample of pond water. Place a small amount in a petri dish.

2 Look for movement of tiny living things. Use a medicine dropper to place 1-2 drops of pond water onto a depression slide. (Picture C)

> **Predict: *What kinds of living things are you likely to see in the pond water?***

3 Place the slide on the stage of a microscope, and examine it under low and high power. Draw a picture of any living things that you see. You may wish to use a reference book to help identify the living things. Record their names on your chart. (Picture C)

State Your Conclusions

1. How do the animals from the soil compare with the animals from the pond water?

2. Did you find any one kind of living thing in both soil and pond water?

Record Your Results

Soil	Pond Water

Let's Experiment

Now that you have explored soil and water, do you think the air contains any tiny living things? Place one slice of fresh bread in a sealable plastic bag. Place another slice on a counter for an hour, and then put it in a second bag. Moisten both pieces of bread with sterilized water. Observe for one week. Use what you know about scientific methods to find out what happens.

3.2 *A Living Planet*

▶ ***Can plants grow in the ocean?***

Imagine you're on a raft in the ocean. All around you stretches an unbroken view of water, water, water. There are no trees, no bushes, no flowers— not even a blade of grass. Could anything grow in this huge, wet world?

The answer is floating right next to your raft. If you look at just one drop of ocean water under a microscope, you'll see hundreds of individual, tiny, living things. All those tiny things live together in a floating carpet of life. This living carpet floats on or near the surface of most of the earth's oceans.

▼ *Below, left: Adult acorn barnacles*
Center: Gooseneck barnacles with feet extended
Below, right: Enlarged photo of a water flea

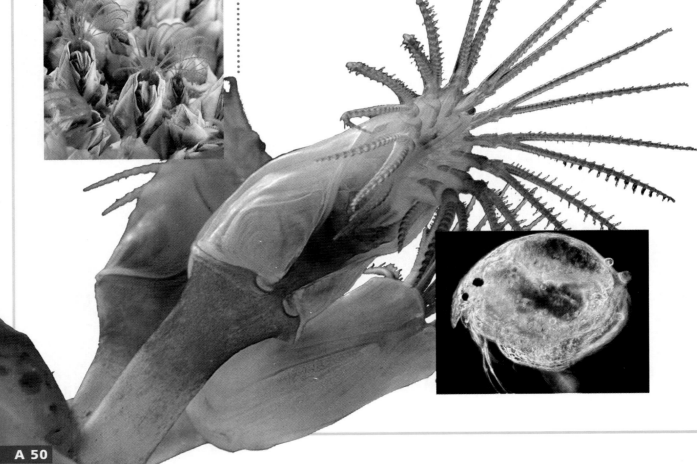

▲ *In the shallow, well-lit water of this tide pool many different kinds of living things thrive.*

These tiny living things are called plankton. They float near the surface of oceans where they get sunlight. They can also be found in tide pools like the one shown above.

The many types of plankton are not the only kinds of living things found in the biosphere. In this lesson you will learn about the incredible variety of life found in the different areas of the biosphere.

The Living Shores

All along the seashore the salty ocean waves meet the land. The waves carry more than water. Some tiny organisms roll in with the waves. Some attach to the rocks along the shore as the waves slide back into the ocean. Barnacles, for example, begin their lives as floating eggs. When the eggs hatch in the ocean water, the baby barnacles drift as they begin to grow. When the water brings a barnacle near a rock, it glues itself to the rock. Then it grows a shell. Find the feet of one of the gooseneck barnacles in the picture. Barnacles eat by extending their legs outside the shell. The legs catch bits of plankton that come in with each new wave. Then the food is passed into the barnacle's mouth inside its shell. When the wave has gone, barnacles are left high and dry on their rocks. But, their shells keep them from drying out in the sunny air.

Water Habitats

Can certain animals live in fresh water? Let's investigate and find out.

What To Do
A. Cut the tops off of two empty plastic 2-liter bottles.
B. Label one bottle "fresh water" and fill it with tap water that has been sitting out for a day.
C. Label the second bottle "salt water" and fill it with the salt water prepared by your teacher.
D. Add 1/2 spoonful of brine shrimp eggs to each bottle.
E. Observe the bottles each day for the next five days. Record what you see taking place in each bottle. A magnifying lens may help.

	Daily Movement				
	1	2	3	4	5
Fresh water					
Salt water					

What Did You Find Out?
1. *In which liquid did the eggs hatch into small brine shrimp?*
2. *Can brine shrimp live in fresh water?*

Into The Field

How many types of living things can you observe?

Observe the outdoors for 10 minutes. Make a list of as many living things as you can find. Compare your list with someone else's.

The Diversity of Life

The gooseneck barnacle is just one kind of living thing. About one and one-half million different types of living things in the biosphere have been identified. Millions more might exist that have not yet been discovered. The picture below shows just some of the diversity found in the animal world. Some life forms, such as bacteria, are so small you can only see them under microscopes. Others, like giant redwood trees of California, can be as tall as 30-story buildings. Some, like polar bears, live in bitter cold polar regions. Others, such as colorful parrots, live in the sweltering heat of rainforests. From the tops of mountains to the dark bottoms of the ocean, life exists.

The Nepalese swift, for example, soars above some of the highest mountains in the world, more than 6 kilometers above sea level. It often flies with its mouth wide open catching any insects that cross its lofty path.

➤ The students in the photo are holding a greenwing macaw, a red-tail boa, and Molly the cat.

Far below the Nepalese swift, the blue lanternfish swims through the deep, deep water of the ocean. The days here are the same as the nights—pitch-black. But the darkness is no problem for the lanternfish. The fish has special organs that give off light.

Life abounds in the ocean. But much of it we can't see. It's easier for us to see the plants and animals of the land around us, such as oak trees. These lovely plants spread their green leaves far above our heads. They provide both shade and fresh air. Acorns from the oak trees fall to the ground. Other oak trees will grow from them and join the biosphere.

Sharing the Sphere

You, your friends, and all the people of Earth are members of just one kind of living thing. We are called *Homo sapiens*. Look at all the living things in the picture on page 52. We share a place in the biosphere with them and with all the other living things on Earth.

Like all other living things, we depend on the biosphere. Without the biosphere, we couldn't exist.

▼ *This bumblebee is searching for nectar on the flower of a thistle.*

▲ *This fish is one of many living things found in the biosphere.*

Checkpoint

1. In which sphere does the gooseneck barnacle live?
2. How do the Nepalese swift and the blue lanternfish survive where they live?
3. Living things are very different from one another, but how are they alike?
4. **Take Action!** Collect pictures of different living things. What helps each survive in its part of the biosphere?

Activity

How Many Living Things Can You Find in a Square Meter?

As you look around your schoolyard, you probably see many living things. But what might you find if you take an even closer look?

Picture A

Picture B

Picture C

Gather These Materials

meter stick
4 wooden stakes
string

large sheet of drawing
paper
pencil

Follow This Procedure

1 Make a chart like the one on the next page. Record your observations in your chart.

2 Select an area of the schoolyard to investigate.

3 Use a meter stick to measure off 1 m on the ground. Push a wooden stake into the ground at each end of the length of the meter. Connect the stakes with string. (Picture A)

4 Measure off the rest of a square, and mark with two more stakes in the other corners. Tie the string around the remaining stakes to form a square. (Picture B)

5 The area inside the stakes and string is 1 square meter of space. Make a pencil drawing of your living square meter on a large sheet of drawing paper.

Predict: *What kinds of organisms will you find in your square meter?*

Record Your Results

Kinds of living things	Observations	Approximate number
Plant life		
Small animals (insects, worms, etc.)		
Larger animals (birds, frogs, etc.)		

6 Carefully examine every part of your square meter. Turn over rocks and look on the underside of leaves. Make a list of all the living things and nonliving things you find on your chart. Count or estimate the number of organisms in each category. (Picture C)

7 Look at your living square meter a week later. How has it changed? Which animals really make their home there? Which are just feeding or passing through?

State Your Conclusions

1. How do your lists compare to your predictions?
2. Which living things are the most common in your square meter?
3. Use your lists to show how the plants and animals are dependent on one another.

Let's Experiment

Now that you have observed the organisms that live in your square meter of space, do you think the same group of organisms live in your space as the seasons change? Use what you know about scientific methods to find out.

Observing

At a large library, you can find hundreds of books about all kinds of animals. Where does that information come from? How do we know so much about animals and other living things? Scientists learn about living things mostly by observing them. When scientists observe, they use their senses to gather as much information as they can. Observing is an important skill that you can sharpen every day.

Thinking It Through

Suppose you had an assignment to gather as much information as you could about a squirrel by observing it. One quick look might tell you that it's a small, brown animal with a bushy tail. But there's more to observing than that. Here's a list of questions you might ask yourself as you take time to observe the squirrel.

1. How would I describe this animal to someone who's never seen one?
2. What can I say about the looks of its paws, legs, head, nose, and so on?
3. How does it move? Does it walk slowly, hop, run, or jump?
4. Does it make any sounds I can hear? How would I describe those sounds?
5. Where does this animal spend its time? How much of its time is spent in trees? in bushes? in open areas?
6. How does it spend its time?
7. How much of its time is spent gathering food?

Your Turn

Now, use questions like these to observe a squirrel, bird, insect, or other animal in your area. You might think of other questions. Write your observations in a journal.

Chapter Review

Thinking Back

1. What would be missing for life on Earth if one of the three spheres was missing?

2. Explain how the sun's energy moves water from one sphere to another.

3. Which spheres are part of the **biosphere?**

4. Why are the **atmosphere**, **hydrosphere**, and **lithosphere** called a system?

5. What are some of the ways living things on Earth are different?

6. In what way does the system of spheres make life on Earth possible?

Connecting Ideas

1. Copy the concept map. Use the terms at the right to complete the map about the biosphere.

atmosphere   **hydrosphere**
lithosphere

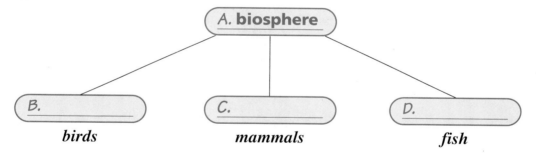

2. Write a sentence or two about the ideas shown in the concept map.

Gathering Evidence

1. In the Activity on page 48, what led you to conclude that life exists in each sphere of the biosphere?

2. In the Activity on page 54, what made you decide how many different kinds of living things existed in your schoolyard?

Doing Science!

1. **Design an activity** that would show the special qualities of the hydrosphere, lithosphere, and the atmosphere.

2. **Create a display** that shows the type of life you might find in each part of the biosphere.

Kids in the Ground Crew

NASA is working with new scientists down here on the earth: kids! Students in kindergarten through twelfth grade have been helping the space agency. This partnership helps both sides. NASA gets a lot of new scientific data, while the kids learn earth and space science.

Some of these space seeds grew as much as four times bigger or faster than the ordinary seeds.

In one NASA activity, over 125,000 classes across the country planted tomato seeds that were given to them by NASA. This may not sound very exciting. But these were special seeds. They had spent almost six years in outer space! They had been kept aboard a U.S. spacecraft.

NASA asked the kids to help figure out if these space seeds would grow differently from seeds that had never left the earth. So the young scientists planted the space seeds next to ordinary seeds. They compared how the seeds grew. Kids from Stuart Elementary School in Patrick County, Virginia, had something interesting to report. They said that the space seeds grew much faster, bigger, and greener than the ordinary seeds. Some of these space seeds grew as much as four times bigger or faster than the ordinary seeds.

In another NASA activity, a group of Global Change programs were set up by the Aspen Global Change Institute of Colorado. This institute's goal is to teach kids how to gather information on the environment. For instance, kids may learn how to measure and track conditions of their town's streams and lakes. Or they may learn how to record air pollution near their community. This information can be compared with data collected about the earth by NASA satellites. By doing this work, kids gain an understanding of their local environment. They see how it is affected by changes around the world.

At the Jenison Junior High School in Michigan, the program has already begun. Students have used their own measurements, along with NASA's aerial photos, to examine how their town's natural landscape has changed.

So far, the Global Change program has been set up in only 12 schools. But it will soon expand to 60 schools. These schools will be all across the United States and in other parts of the world.

On Your Own

1. Write to NASA if you would like your school to participate in the space seed program.

2. You can find out how the water you drink is cleaned by visiting a water treatment plant. Find out where the water comes from and what kinds of pollution in your environment affect the water that you drink.

An Engineer in Space

Dr. Ellen Ochoa

Occupation: Astronaut
Hobbies: Playing the flute
Goals: To help build a space station and to go on a return trip to the moon

Your safety belts are strapped. All systems are go. The engines roar. You try to remain calm. Four, three, two, one, blast-off!

Can you imagine what it would be like to fly to the moon? Lots of kids dream of becoming an astronaut. But Ellen Ochoa never did. "When I was growing up, there were no female astronauts. So it never occurred to me that I could be one." That's all changed now. Today, Ellen is one of seventeen female astronauts.

Who gets to be an astronaut?

About 2000 people apply for each class. And only about twenty are chosen. Ellen was one of the lucky ones. She thinks it's because she's always worked hard—at school and at her job. Her first job was being an engineer.

Does being an engineer help?

Ellen works with laser computers. They can solve problems that people usually handle. For example, imagine playing with a remote-control car. What would happen if you couldn't see where the car was going? It might crash into things. Now imagine a spacecraft, with no people on board, landing on Mars. A laser computer could guide the spacecraft to the perfect landing site.

Why did you want to be an astronaut?

"As a researcher I always enjoyed discovering things for myself. The space program is the only way to leave Earth and see for yourself what's out there."

What do you like best about being an astronaut?

"There's lots of variety. I work on the simulator and train for missions. When you train, you're given many unexpected problems. Then everyone in the crew works together to solve the problems."

Space Suit: Heavy Protection

One thing is certain—if you wanted to leave the earth's atmosphere, you would have to take along everything the air does for you just to stay alive. All the equipment you would need might weigh as much as 112 kilograms.

1 The primary life support system is worn like a backpack. It contains all the control systems and oxygen for breathing and for air pressure.

2 Astronauts talk to each other and to Control Central using microphones and headphones. They transmit their messages on a radio.

3 The helmet is covered by a solar shield that filters the sun and protects from excessive heat.

4 The gloves have silicone fingertips to give some sensitivity.

5 Since there is no gravity, an astronaut working outside the spacecraft must be attached to the craft to keep from floating away.

Find Out On Your Own

Write a letter to an astronaut asking him or her to describe the characteristics and functions of a space suit.

Module Review

Making Connections

Systems and Interactions

1. How does gravity affect the interaction between the sun and the planets?

2. Give an example of how the Earth and moon system and the Earth and sun system interact and explain why.

Diversity

3. In what ways do the inner planets differ?

4. What are some unique factors that enable Earth to support life?

Using What I Learned

Comparing

1. Compare Venus, Mercury, and Earth, and explain how their atmospheres affect the ability to sustain life.

Predicting

2. If you knew that a planet had a very thin atmosphere, what could you predict about life on that planet?

Categorizing

3. Name the physical characteristics you can use to classify the area of the biosphere in which an animal lives.

Communicating

4. Draw a diagram that shows how water moves through the biosphere.

Ordering

5. What would be the order of Earth, moon, and sun from the object with the most to least mass?

Applying

6. Why might humans wear masks and flippers when swimming?

Relating

7. What causes the three spheres of the biosphere to form a system? Explain why.

Observing

8. Tell in which sphere or spheres of the biosphere the animals in the pictures would live and how you would know.

Applying What I Learned

Action Project

Make a survey of the pets that people living in your community have. Find out in which sphere or spheres of the biosphere they live.

Drawing

Make a drawing to show the diversity of life in each sphere of the biosphere.

Science Theater

Prepare a skit for a news show describing the discovery of a new planet. Explain what type of atmosphere it has, its orbit, and whether life is possible.

Performance Task

Use a flashlight, a table tennis ball, and a larger ball to symbolize the sun, moon, and Earth to show how a solar and lunar eclipse occur and how they affect light.

Exhibition

Make a poster or bulletin board comparing two or more of the planets in the solar system.

What If

What if a nearby marsh, forest, or open land were to be made into a shopping center? What questions might you ask concerning the effect this might have on plants and animals in that area?

Using Metric

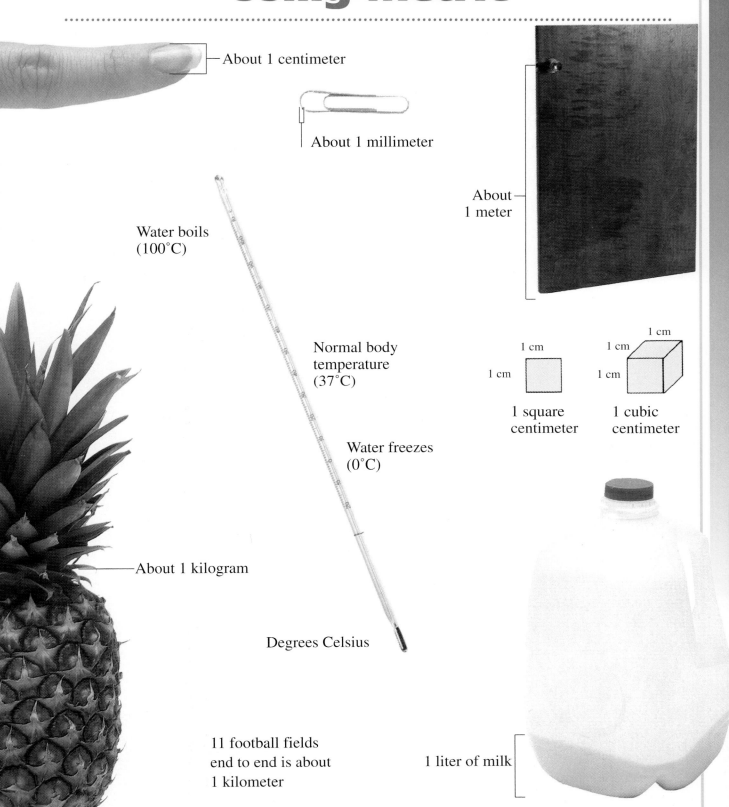

About 1 centimeter

About 1 millimeter

About 1 meter

Water boils (100°C)

Normal body temperature (37°C)

1 cm
1 cm
1 square centimeter

1 cm
1 cm
1 cm
1 cm
1 cubic centimeter

Water freezes (0°C)

About 1 kilogram

Degrees Celsius

11 football fields end to end is about 1 kilometer

1 liter of milk

Using Scientific Methods

Scientists ask many questions. No one may know the answers. Then scientists use scientific methods to find answers. Scientific methods include steps like those on the next page. Scientists sometimes use the steps in different order. You can use these steps to do the experiments in this section.

Test Hypothesis If possible, experiments are done to test the hypothesis. Experiments should be repeated to double check the results.

Collect Data The information you gather from the experiment is your data.

Study Data The data collected during an experiment is better understood if it is organized into charts and graphs. Then you can easily see what it all means.

Make Conclusions The conclusion relates to the hypothesis. You might conclude your hypothesis is correct, or that it is incorrect.

Identify Problem The problem is usually in the form of a question such as, "How much space does a bean plant need to grow best?"

Make Observations Recorded observations become data and might include the size, color, or shape of something.

State Hypothesis A hypothesis is a likely explanation of the problem. It may turn out to be incorrect; it must be tested.

Safety in Science

Scientists do their experiments safely. You need to be careful when doing experiments too. The next page includes some safety tips to remember.

- Read each experiment carefully.

- Wear cover goggles when needed.

- Clean up spills right away.

- Never taste or smell substances unless directed to do so by your teacher.

- Tape sharp edges of materials.

- Put things away when you finish an experiment.

- Wash your hands after each experiment.

Experiment Skills

Identifying a Problem

Experimenting with the Size of Splashes

Matt spilled some tomato juice when he poured a glass of juice for his little brother. Some juice landed on the table. More juice fell to the floor. Matt wondered why the splashes on the floor were much bigger than the splashes on the table.

Matt had identified a problem: What causes drops of a liquid to make splashes of different sizes? He knew that gravity was acting on all the drops. Gravity is the force that pulled the drops downward. Also, he believed that all the drops he spilled were about the same size. Matt decided to do an experiment to solve his problem.

Thinking About the Experiment

Matt could think of only one difference between the drops that hit the table and those that hit the floor. The drops that hit the floor had a greater distance to fall.

1. Which tomato juice drops fell from a greater distance?

2. Which tomato juice drops made bigger splashes?

3. What might Matt conclude from these observations?

In science class, Matt had learned that the variable being tested is the part of an experiment that changes. Also, a control is a part of the experiment that does not have the variable being tested.

4. What is the variable being tested in Matt's experiment on the next page?

5. What parts of Matt's experiment do not change?

Try It!
Try Matt's experiment and see if you come to the same conclusion.

Problem
What causes drops of a liquid to make splashes of different sizes?

Hypothesis
The size of the splash made by a drop is related to the distance the drop falls.

Materials
large sheet of
   white paper
cup
water
food coloring
dropper
meter stick

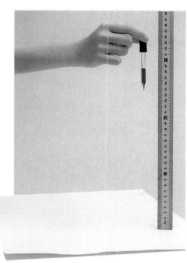

Procedure
1. Fill a cup halfway with water.

2. Add a few drops of food coloring to the water.

3. Lay the paper on the floor.

4. Fill the dropper halfway with colored water.

5. Stand the meter stick up on the paper. Set the stick so it is near one end of the paper. Hold the dropper 25 cm above the paper.

6. Drop 1 drop of colored water on the paper from a height of 25 cm. Write 25 cm on the paper next to the splash.

7. Move the stick a small distance away from the splash.

8. Repeat steps 5 and 6 at heights of 50 cm and 100 cm. After each drop, write the height of the drop next to the splash. Then move the meter stick so there is space on the paper for the next drop.

Data and Observations
Tell what happened to the size of the splash. In a chart like the one below, write: small, bigger, biggest.

Distance	Size of splash
25 cm	
50 cm	
100 cm	

Conclusion
Write your conclusion based on your data and observations.

Practice

Identifying a Problem
1. Suppose you wanted to do an experiment that compared the thickness of liquids to the size of their splashes. Identify the problem you would want to solve in your experiment.
2. How would you change Matt's experiment to solve this problem?

Experiment Skills
Testing a Hypothesis

Experimenting with Gravity

When the noon bell rang, Tom dropped his apple core into an empty paper cup. On the way out of the lunch room, he pitched the paper cup into a wastebasket. He noticed that the apple core stayed in the cup and landed in the basket—still inside the cup. Tom wondered why the apple core did not fly out of the cup before the cup hit the basket.

Tom had observed many falling objects. He wondered about how the force of gravity affects objects that are falling at the same time. He thought that objects falling together fall at the same rate.

Tom decided to set up an experiment with falling objects. He watched a cup of water fall. Then he poked holes in another cup. He put water into this cup and observed it as it fell.

Thinking About the Experiment
Tom dropped a cup and water to test his hypothesis. He observed the rate at which each fell.

1. What was Tom's hypothesis?

2. What might Tom have observed if the water fell slower than the cup? faster?

Tom observed that water did not flow out of cup 2 when the holes were uncovered and the cup was dropped.

3. What does this tell you about the rate at which the water and cup fell?

4. What does this tell you about Tom's hypothesis?

Try It!

Try Tom's experiment and see if you come to the same conclusion.

Problem

How does the force of gravity affect objects falling together?

Hypothesis

Write your own hypothesis for this experiment.

Materials

2 paper cups
  of the same size
sink or large pail

pencil
tap water
meter stick

Procedure

1 Label the cups *1* and *2*.

2 Fill cup *1* half full of water.

3 Hold the cup at least 1 m above a sink or pail. Let go of the cup and observe what happens to it and the water as the cup falls. Record your observations.

4 Use the point of a pencil to make two small holes near the center of the bottom of cup *2*.

5 Cover the holes in the cup with your fingers. Then fill cup *2* halfway with water.

6 Hold the cup at least 1 m above a sink or pail. Take your finger off the holes. Observe what happens to the water. Record your observations.

7 Again fill cup *2* half full of water, holding your fingers over the holes. Hold the cup over a sink or pail. Uncover the holes as you let go of the cup. Observe what happens to the water and the cup as the cup falls. Record your observations.

Data and Observations

Situation	Observations
Cup 1 (falling)	
Cup 2 (held)	
Cup 2 (falling)	

Conclusion

Write your conclusion based on your data and observations.

Practice

Testing a Hypothesis

Suppose you wanted to find out how the force of gravity affects the water in a cup with holes on the side.

1. What would your hypothesis be?

2. How could you set up an experiment to test your hypothesis?

3. What experiment results would support your hypothesis?

Setting Up a Control

Experimenting with Salt Water

Alex was on a vacation with his family. He noticed that it seemed easier to float in the ocean than in the pool back home. Alex knew that ocean water has salt in it. His pool was filled with water from a faucet. This water is fresh water and is not salty.

Alex wondered if things float more easily in salt water than in fresh water. Alex decided to set up an experiment to find out. He filled a cup with salt water. Alex added drops of colored fresh water, vinegar, and rubbing alcohol to the salt water. Alex then watched to see whether the drops floated or sank.

Thinking About the Experiment
Review what Alex wanted to do.

1. What was the problem Alex wanted to solve?

2. Write a hypothesis for the problem.

Alex did not set up his experiment correctly. He did not have a control. The control is the part of the experiment that does not have the variable being tested.

3. Could Alex compare whether the liquids floated more easily in salt water than in fresh water? Explain.

4. What type of water should have been the control?

5. Read Alex's experiment on the next page. How did Alex correct his experiment to have a control?

Try It!

Try Alex's experiment and see if you come to the same conclusion.

Problem

Do things float more easily in salt water than in fresh water?

Hypothesis

Write your own hypothesis for this experiment.

Materials

graduated cylinder   white vinegar
salt   rubbing alcohol
food coloring   1 small plastic cup
water   3 droppers
2 large plastic cups spoon

Procedure

1. Label one large cup *Fresh water* and the other large cup *Salt water.*

2. Add 200 mL of tap water to each of the large cups.

3. Pour 50 mL of salt into the cup labeled *Salt water.* Stir the salt until it dissolves.

4. Pour 5 mL of fresh water into the small cup. Add several drops of food coloring.

5. Add one or two drops of the colored water to the *Fresh water* cup. Observe what happens to the drops.

6. Now add one or two drops of the colored water to the *Salt water* cup. Observe what happens to the drops. Rinse all the cups.

7. Repeat steps 2 through 6, using colored vinegar instead of colored water in the small cup.

8. Repeat steps 2 through 6, using colored alcohol instead of colored water in the small cup.

Data and Observations

Do the drops mix, float, or sink?

	Fresh water	Salt water
Water		
Alcohol		
Vinegar		

Conclusion

Write your conclusion based on your data and observations.

Testing a Hypothesis

MODULE B

Experimenting with Brine Shrimp

Terry went to a pet store to get some brine shrimp to feed to his fish. He enjoyed looking at all the fish while he was there. Terry noticed that the store owner kept brine shrimp in an aquarium under bright light. He wondered why. He thought of a hypothesis to explain what he noticed: Brine shrimp like light places more than dark places. Terry decided to do an experiment to test his hypothesis.

He bought some brine shrimp and put them in a clear plastic jar. He cut a small hole in a piece of black paper. He wrapped the paper around the jar so that the hole would let light into part of the jar. Then he shined a flashlight through the hole. He took off the paper and observed the brine shrimp.

Thinking About the Experiment
Terry made an observation in the pet store that made him wonder about brine shrimp. Then he thought of a hypothesis.

1. What did Terry notice?

2. What was Terry's hypothesis?

To test his hypothesis, Terry first put the hole in the paper near the bottom of a jar and made observations. Then he moved the hole near the top of the jar and made observations.

3. How did using black paper help Terry test his hypothesis?

4. Why was it important for him to shine the light in two different places?

5. If the brine shrimp had gathered only at the bottom of the jar, would Terry's hypothesis have been correct? Why?

Try It!

Try Terry's experiment and see if you come to the same conclusion.

Problem

Do brine shrimp like light places or dark places?

Hypothesis

Brine shrimp like light places more than dark places.

Materials

20 brine shrimp   scissors
plastic jar   flashlight
black paper   clock or watch
tape   with second hand

Procedure

1 Put the brine shrimp and salt water in a clear plastic jar.

2 Cut a piece of black paper large enough to wrap around the jar. Cut a small square out of one edge of the paper.

3 Wrap the paper around the jar so that the square hole is near the bottom of the jar. Use tape to hold the paper in place. If the lid of the jar is clear, cover it with black paper.

4 Shine the flashlight through the hole for about 1 minute.

5 Quickly remove the paper and observe where the brine shrimp are. Record your observations in a chart like the one below.

6 Repeat steps 3-5, but position the paper so the square hole is near the top of the jar.

Data and Observations

	Position of Shrimp
Light at bottom	
Light at top	

Conclusion

Write your conclusion based on your data and observations.

Practice

Testing a Hypothesis

1. Suppose you put some warm salt water in the jar. Then you put a funnel in the warm water and pour cold salt water through the funnel. When you remove the funnel, the cold salt water will stay under the warm salt water. You put brine shrimp in the jar and observe their behavior. What is the variable being tested in this new procedure?

2. What hypothesis are you testing?

Setting Up an Experiment

Experimenting with Erosion

Robin lives where winter brings ice and snow. One spring, she saw that some soil had washed away from the hill behind her house. No soil had washed away in her front yard. Her front yard was flat. Robin wondered whether the slope of the land affected the amount of erosion caused by melting ice and snow. She thought it did.

Robin wanted to do an experiment to find out. She needed a way to set up models of flat land and a hill. She decided to use damp sand for soil. She found two lids from shoe boxes to hold the sand. She decided to use ice cubes for melting ice and snow.

Thinking About the Experiment

1. What is the problem that Robin wants to solve?

2. Write a hypothesis for the problem.

The experiment on the next page describes how Robin set up her experiment. She kept every part of the setup the same except for one part. This part is the variable she wanted to test.

3. What parts of the setup are the same for each model?

4. What is the variable Robin's setup tests?

Robin also has a control in her experiment. The control is the part of the setup that shows what happens when ice melts on soil that has no slope.

5. Which part of the setup is the control?

6. What does the part of the setup with the hill of sand test?

Try It!

Try Robin's experiment and see if you come to the same conclusion.

Problem

Does the slope of land affect the amount of erosion caused by melting ice?

Hypothesis

Write your own hypothesis for this experiment.

Materials

2 lids from shoe boxes
aluminum foil
damp sand
2 ice cubes

Procedure

1 Cover the inside of both lids with foil to make them waterproof.

2 Fill each lid with the same amount of damp sand.

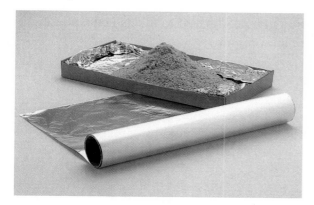

3 In 1 lid, shape a steep hill.

4 Smooth out the sand in the other lid so that it is flat.

5 Place 1 ice cube on top of the hill. Place another ice cube in the middle of the flat sand.

6 Watch as the ice melts in each lid. Record your observations in a chart like the one below.

Data and Observations

	Amount of Erosion
Flat land	
Hill	

Conclusion

Write your conclusion based on your data and observations.

Practice

Setting Up an Experiment

1. If you wanted to set up an experiment to find out how the slope of land affects erosion caused by rain, what would be your hypothesis?
2. Describe how you would set up the experiment to test your hypothesis.

Using Models

MODULE C

Experimenting with Properties of Liquids and Solids

Tim's science class was studying earthquakes. He learned that the earth's plates float on partly melted rock, which is located deep inside the earth. This partly melted rock makes up a layer of the earth called the asthenosphere.

Tim read that the asthenosphere is subjected to tremendous pressure and heat. Because of these conditions, rock in the asthenosphere can flow like a very thick liquid.

Tim searched for some ordinary material that shows properties of both a liquid and a solid. He wanted to use this material to make a model of the asthenosphere. He learned that adding water to cornstarch creates a substance with unusual properties. He decided to use cornstarch for his model.

Thinking About the Experiment

In order for a model to be useful, it must show how something looks or works. Scientists use models to describe ideas about nature. They often use a model to represent something, such as the asthenosphere, which they cannot see directly.

1. In the procedure on the next page, describe the point where the mixture best represents the asthenosphere.

2. Would the model be more like a liquid or a solid in step 3? in step 6?

3. What would the nail show?

4. In what part of the procedure could the model be compared to the asthenosphere under pressure?

Try It!

Try Tim's experiment and see if you come to the same conclusion.
....

Problem

Do some materials have properties of both liquids and solids?

Hypothesis

Some materials have properties of both liquids and solids.

Materials

balance
cornstarch, (40 g)
nail
water

clear plastic cup
graduated cylinder
spoon

Procedure

1 Pour 15 mL of water into a cup.

2 Mix 10 g of cornstarch in the cup.

3 Place the nail head-first on the surface of the mixture. Observe the consistency of the mixture and whether it can support the nail. Record your observations.

4 Add 5 g more of cornstarch to the bowl and stir until it is mixed. Repeat step 3.

5 Repeat step 4 until the mixture is thick enough to be scooped up and rolled into a small ball. Record your observations.

6 Put the ball of cornstarch mixture in the palm of your hand. Let it warm on your palm for several minutes. Record any changes you see.

7 Remold the mixture into a ball. Apply gentle pressure to the ball for several minutes. Observe and record how the ball responds to pressure.

Data and Observations

Amount of cornstarch	Texture of mixture	Effect on nail
10 g		
15 g		
20 g		
25 g		
30 g		

	Changes in ball shape
In palm	
With pressure	

Conclusion

Write your conclusion based on your data and observations.

Practice

Using Models

Suppose you wanted to find out if a mixture of flour and water has the properties of both a liquid and a solid and can be used to make a model of the asthenosphere.

1. What would be your hypothesis?

2. How would you set up an experiment to test your hypothesis?

3. What would be the model in the experiment?

Setting Up an Experiment

MODULE D

Experimenting with Yeast

Glen was helping his aunt make bread. The recipe called for yeast. His aunt told him that yeast are one-celled organisms. They use an ingredient in the recipe for food. When they use food, they make a gas that causes the bread dough to rise. Glen wondered what ingredient the yeast use for food. The recipe listed flour, sugar, salt, water, eggs, and yeast. Glen wondered if yeast might use sugar for food.

He decided to set up an experiment to find out if yeast use sugar. Since yeast make a gas when they use food, he decided to set up an experiment that would show if gas was given off. By putting balloons over the mouths of jars, Glen can tell if the yeast are using food. The gas they make will help blow up the balloons.

Thinking About the Experiment

1. What is the problem that Glen wants to solve?

2. Write a hypothesis for the problem.

Read Glen's experiment carefully. He kept every part of the setup the same except for one part. This part is the variable he was testing.

3. What did he put in each jar?

4. What parts of the setup are the same for each jar?

5. What is the variable that changes in the setup?

Glen also has a control in his experiment. The control is the part of the setup that shows what happens to the balloon when yeast do not have any food.

6. Which part of the setup is the control?

7. What does the part of the setup with sugar test?

Try It!

Try Glen's experiment and see if you come to the same conclusion.

Problem
What do yeast use for food?

Hypothesis
Write your own hypothesis for this experiment.

Materials
2 identical jars with small mouths
cover goggles
tape
spoonful of sugar

2 spoonfuls of yeast
20 mL warm water
2 balloons

Procedure
1. Put a piece of tape on each of the jars. Write *No food* on 1 piece of tape. Write *Sugar* on another piece of tape.

2. Put a spoonful of sugar in the jar labeled *Sugar.*

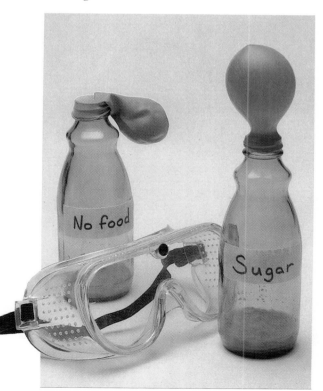

3. Put a spoonful of yeast in each jar.

4. Add 10 mL of warm water to each jar.

5. Stretch a balloon over the mouth of each jar.

6. Place the jars in a warm, dark place for the night.

7. The next day observe the balloons. Record the observations in a chart like the one below.

Data and Observations
Descriptions of balloons

	Changes in balloons
Sugar	
No food	

Conclusion
Write your conclusion based on your data and observations.

Practice

Setting Up an Experiment
1. If you wanted to do an experiment to find out if yeast use sugar or corn syrup better as food, what might be your hypothesis?
2. Describe how you would set up the experiment to test your hypothesis.

Testing a Hypothesis

Experimenting with Water

Tina was getting ice cubes from the freezer. She noticed that the water in the tray that had been filled with water was not frozen. The water in the tray that had been only half full was frozen. Tina remembered that during the winter small ponds freeze sooner than larger lakes. In both examples, the water that did not freeze as fast had a larger volume. Tina decided that a larger volume of water cools more slowly than a smaller volume of water.

Tina wanted to test her hypothesis. She decided to use a large and a small jar to stand for a pond and a lake. She used a thermometer to measure how fast warm water cooled in each jar.

Thinking About the Experiment

The experiment on the next page describes how Tina tested her hypothesis.

1. How are the two jars of water alike?

2. How are they different?

3. Tina could have tested her hypothesis using two jars of the same size. Explain how the jars could still have different volumes.

4. Why did Tina begin with warm water?

In an experiment, the part that is different between setups is the variable being tested.

5. What variable is being tested in Tina's experiment?

6. Why did Tina measure the water temperature in both jars at the same time?

Try It!

Try Tina's experiment and see if you come to the same conclusion.

Problem

How does the amount of water affect how fast the water loses heat?

Hypothesis

A larger volume of water cools more slowly than a smaller volume does.

Materials

1 small plastic jar warm tap water
l large plastic jar clock or watch
2 thermometers   with second hand

Procedure

1 Fill both jars with warm tap water.

2 Place each jar on a flat surface, about 15 cm apart.

3 Place a thermometer in each jar.

4 Use a clock or watch to time each minute.

5 Read the water temperature in each jar once each minute for the next 10 minutes. Record the temperatures in a chart like the one shown.

Data and Observations

Time in minutes	Temperature in °C	
	Large jar	Small jar
0		
1		
2		
3		
4		
5		
6		
7		
8		
9		
10		

Conclusion

Write your conclusion based on your data and observations.

Practice

Testing a Hypothesis

Another experiment would be needed to find out if large bodies of water warm up faster than smaller ones.

1. Write a hypothesis for this experiment.

2. How could you change the experiment above to test this hypothesis?

Setting Up an Experiment

Experimenting with Evaporation

Julie's science class made salt solutions on Friday. When the bell rang, the students put their jars of solution in a cupboard. Julie left her jar on a sunny windowsill in the classroom.

On Monday, Julie found that only salt crystals were left in her jar. The water had evaporated from her solution. She noticed that the jars in the cupboard still contained solutions. Julie decided that the warm temperature on the windowsill caused her solution to evaporate quickly.

She set up an experiment to see how temperature affects the evaporation of salt water. She left jars of salt water open to air at different temperatures.

Thinking About the Experiment

Julie knew that water slowly disappears if it is left in an open container.

1. What happened to the water in Julie's solution?

2. How could she have kept her solution from evaporating?

3. Could Julie have set up her experiment, shown on the next page, using tap water instead of salt water? Explain.

Julie set up her experiment so that only one thing is different for the jars. The part of the experiment that is different is the variable being tested.

4. What is the same for each jar?

5. What is the variable begin tested in Julie's experiment?

Julie has a control in her experiment. In this experiment, the control is the part of the setup that shows how fast water evaporates in Julie's classroom. Note procedure step 4.

6. Which part of the setup is the control?

Try It!

Try Julie's experiment and see if you come to the same conclusion.

Problem

Does the temperature of the air have an effect on how fast salt water evaporates from an open container?

Hypothesis

Salt water evaporates faster in warm air than in cold air.

Materials

3 jars of same size   water
salt   marker
spoon   200-watt lamp
graduated cylinder   and stand

Procedure

1 Use the marker to label the 3 jars *A*, *B*, and *C*.

2 Prepare a salt solution by dissolving 5 mL of salt in 60 mL of warm water.

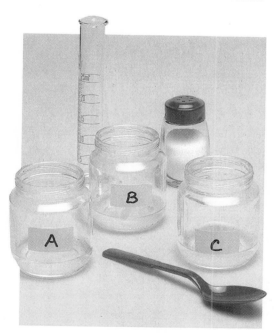

3 Pour 20 mL of the salt solution into each of the 3 jars. Mark the water level on the side of each jar.

4 Set jar *A* under the lighted lamp. Place jar *B* somewhere in the room where it will not be disturbed. Set jar *C* in a cold place. Make sure none of the jars is in a drafty place.

5 Check the jars at the end of each day for 3 days. Record your observations in a chart like the one below.

Data and Observations

Day	Water level		
	A	B	C
1			
2			
3			

Conclusion

Write your conclusion based on your data and observations.

Practice

Setting Up an Experiment
Suppose you want to find out how air temperature affects the evaporation of a liquid other than salt water.
1. What liquid would you use?
2. What might be your hypothesis?
3. How would you set up an experiment to test your hypothesis?

Experiment Skills
Making Conclusions

··· MODULE E ···

Experimenting with Cotton Thread and Humidity

Jennifer liked to curl her naturally straight hair. She noticed that on dry, cold days her hair stayed curly. On hot, humid days, her curls became looser. Jennifer asked her teacher if human hair shows how much moisture is in the air. The teacher explained that an instrument called a hair hygrometer measures humidity. The hair hygrometer works because hair stretches out when the air becomes humid. The hair absorbs moisture from the air.

Jennifer wondered if she could make a hygrometer from cotton thread. She wondered if the thread would measure relative humidity accurately. She made this hypothesis to answer her question: *A cotton thread hygrometer accurately measures changes in relative humidity.* Jennifer set up an experiment to test her hypothesis.

Thinking About the Experiment
Jennifer collected data in her experiment. She used the data to make a conclusion about the accuracy of her hypothesis. She studied the data to decide if it supported her hypothesis.

1. In the procedure on the next page, what did Jennifer observe to test her hypothesis?

2. On what data would she base her conclusion?

3. What would Jennifer's data and observations have to show in order to support her hypothesis?

The length of the cotton thread did not change. Jennifer concluded that the data she collected did not support her hypothesis.

4. What kind of data would make her conclude that her hypothesis is false?

5. Why did Jennifer need to know the relative humidity of the air?

Try It!

Try Jennifer's experiment and see if you come to the same conclusion.

Problem

Can a cotton thread hygrometer accurately measure changes in the relative humidity of air?

Hypothesis

Recall that Jennifer's hypothesis was incorrect. Write your own hypothesis for this experiment.

Materials

pencil	metric ruler
scissors	shoe box
transparent tape	small nail
cotton thread, 20 cm long	paper, 2 cm x 3 cm

Procedure

1 Fasten the head end of the nail to one end of the thread with small pieces of tape.

2 Tape the other end of the thread to the inside bottom of the shoe box. Tape the thread so it is centered near one end of the box.

3 Stand the shoe box on its end so the thread hangs straight down the middle of the box.

4 Use the ruler to measure 25 mm on the edge of the paper. Mark off every millimeter on the line. Label every 5 mm, starting at 0 mm.

5 Tape the scale to the bottom of the shoe box, beside the nail. The tip of the nail should touch the 13 mm mark.

6 Every day for 5 days record the position of the nail tip on the scale. Try to make your measurements at the same time of day. Record your measurements on a chart like the one shown.

7 Get the actual relative humidity from a local weather report for each time you record the nail's position. Record the actual relative humidity on your chart.

Data and Observations

Date	Position of nail tip	Relative humidity

Conclusion

Write your conclusion based on your data and observations.

Practice

Making Conclusions

Suppose you wanted to test materials other than cotton thread for making a hygrometer.

1. What other materials might you use?
2. If you tested one of those materials and found that during high humidity the materials sometimes got shorter and sometimes got longer, what might you conclude?

Making Conclusions

Experimenting with Grape Ivy Leaves

Shannon visited a sunny greenhouse. She bought a grape ivy plant. The woman at the greenhouse told her that this kind of plant grows best when it gets a lot of light.

When Shannon got home, she began to wonder what would happen to the plant's leaves if they did not get enough light. Before she could make any conclusions, she would need to do an experiment. Shannon chose a large healthy branch with six leaves on it. She taped squares of black paper to the front and back of each leaf. She left the plant near a sunny window.

Thinking About the Experiment

1. Why did Shannon cover some of the leaves?

2. Why did Shannon not cover all of the leaves on the plant?

After a week, Shannon removed the paper from the leaves. Three leaves had turned yellow. Two others had yellow spots. The sixth leaf was a pale green.

3. Should Shannon have concluded that her hypothesis was wrong since one covered leaf still looked green? Explain.

4. What part of Shannon's data supported her hypothesis?

5. What conclusion do you think Shannon reached?

Suppose that Shannon had observed no changes in the leaves that were covered for a week.

6. Would that data support her hypothesis? Explain.

7. What conclusion would Shannon have made based on that data?

Try It!

Try Shannon's experiment and see if you come to the same conclusion.

Problem

What happens to grape ivy leaves when they do not get enough light?

Hypothesis

Leaves of grape ivy plants will not stay green if they do not get enough light.

Materials

2 sheets of black paper
scissors

grape ivy plant
tape
water

Procedure

1 Choose a branch of the plant with 5 or 6 healthy leaves on it.

2 Cut 2 squares of black paper for each leaf on the branch. The squares should be big enough to cover the leaves completely.

3 Tape 2 squares together along 1 edge. Slip a leaf between the 2 squares. Then tape the other edge of the squares together.

4 Put the plant in a sunny place and water it normally.

5 After 1 week, remove the paper from the leaves.

6 Using a chart like the one shown, record how the leaves look.

Data and Observations

	Appearance of leaves
Covered leaves	
Leaves with no color	

Conclusion

Write your conclusion based on your data and observations.

Practice

Making Conclusions

1. If you wanted to experiment to find out if white paper squares block out the same amount of light as black paper squares, how would you change the procedure?
2. If leaves covered with white squares showed no changes, what conclusion would you make?

Glossary

A

adaptation (ad′ap tā′shən), a structure or behavior that helps a living thing live in its surroundings.

adapted (ə dap′tid), made fit to live under certain conditions.

air mass, a large amount of air with the same temperature and humidity.

air pressure (presh′ər), the amount that air presses or pushes on anything.

air resistance (ri zis′təns), a force that slows down the movement of objects through the air.

altitude (al′tə tüd), the height above sea level.

anemometer (an′ə mom′ə tər), a tool that measures wind speed.

asteroid (as′tə roid′), a rocky object orbiting the sun between the planets.

asteroid (as′tə roid′) **belt,** a large group of rocks that orbit the sun between Mars and Jupiter.

atmosphere (at′mə sfir), the layer of gases that surrounds the earth.

atom (at′əm), a basic bit of matter.

axis (ak′sis), an imaginary line through a spinning object.

B

barometer (bə rom′ə tər), an instrument that measures air pressure.

Beaufort (bō′fərt) **scale,** a scale used to estimate wind speed based on observing objects moving in the environment.

biosphere (bī′ə sfir), the region on and surrounding the earth that can support life and that includes the atmosphere, water, and soil.

C

Calorie (kal′ər ē), a specific amount of energy in food.

carbon dioxide (dī ok′sīd), a gas in air that is taken in by plants, exhaled by animals, and given off when fuel is burned.

Celsius (sel′sē əs) **degree,** a unit for measuring temperature.

central vent (sen′trəl vent), a large hole through which magma bursts out of a volcano.

cirrus (sir′əs) **cloud,** a white, feathery cloud made up of tiny pieces of ice.

climate (klī′mit), the average weather conditions of an area over many years.

cold front, the area where a cold air mass moves toward a warm air mass and pushes the warm air up quickly.

colonizer (kol′ə nīz ər), a living thing that comes into an area to eat and live.

comet (kom′it), a frozen chunk of ice and dust that orbits the sun.

compressed (kəm prest′) **air,** air put under extra pressure or squeezed so that it takes up less space.

condense (kən dens′), to change from a gas to a liquid.

conservation (kon′sər vā′shən), protecting from loss or from being used up.

consumer (kən sü′mər), a living thing that depends on producers for food.

contract (kən trakt′), to become smaller in size or to move closer together.

control (kən trol′), the part of an experiment that does not have the variable being tested.

convection (kən vek′shən) **currents,** the circular movement of gases or liquids as a result of differences in temperature.

core (kôr), the center part of the earth.

crust (krust), the top layer of the earth.

cumulonimbus (kyü′myə lō nim′bəs) **cloud,** a cloud that looks like a tall, dark cumulus cloud and often brings thunderstorms.

cumulus (kyü′myə ləs) **cloud,** a white, fluffy cloud that looks like cotton.

D

dark zone, the ocean waters between 1200 and 4000 meters deep where sunlight does not reach.

deciduous (di sij′ü əs) **tree,** one of a group of trees that lose their leaves in the fall.

decomposer (dē′kəm pō′zər), a consumer that puts materials from dead plants and animals back into soil, air, and water.

dissolve (di zolv′), to spread evenly in a liquid and form a solution.

Doppler (dop′lər) **radar,** a type of radar that shows distance and direction of movement.

E

earthquake (ėrth′kwāk), a shaking or sliding of the earth's crust.

ecosystem (ē′kō sis′təm), a community and its nonliving environment.

ellipse (i lips′), the shape of a circle that has been flattened a little.

erosion (i rō′zhən), the moving of weathered rocks and soil by wind, water, or ice.

eruption (i rup′shən), the bursting forth or flowing of lava from a volcano.

evacuate (i vak′yü āt), to withdraw from.

evaporate (i vap′ə rāt′), to change from a liquid to a gas.

evergreen, a plant that stays green all year, including firs and pines.

extinct (ek stingkt′), something that is no longer found living on earth.

F

fault (fôlt), a crack in the earth's crust along which rocks move.

fault-block mountain, a mountain that forms when a big block of rock moves up along a fault.

folded mountain, a mountain that forms when two plates in the earth's crust collide and the edges of the plates crumple.

food chain, the path that energy and nutrients take in a community.

force (fôrs), a push or a pull.

fossil (fos′əl), a trace of a plant or animal that is often found in sedimentary rock.

front, the line where two air masses meet.

G

gas, a state of matter with no definite shape or volume.

geyser (gī′zer), a spring that spouts a fountain or jet of hot water and steam into the air.

glacier (glā′shər), a large mass of ice that moves very slowly.

glider (glī′dər), a motorless aircraft that is kept in the air by rising air currents.

graduated cylinder (graj′ü āt ed sil′ən dər), piece of equipment used for measuring volume.

gravitational force (grav′ə tā′shə nəl fôrs), the pull of gravity that causes all the planets to orbit around the sun.

gravity (grav′ə tē), a force that pulls any two objects together.

greenhouse effect, the trapping of heat by the air around the earth.

H

habitat (hab′ə tat), the place where a living thing lives.

high-pressure area, an area where cool air sinks and pushes down on the earth with more pressure.

Homo sapiens (hō′mō sā′pē enz), the species including all existing races of human beings.

hot spot, a place in the earth's mantle where the mantle melts because of extreme heat.

humidity (hyü mid′ə tē), the amount of water vapor in the air.

hurricane (hėr′ə kān), a huge storm that forms over a warm ocean and has strong winds and heavy rains.

hydrogen (hī′drə jən), a colorless, odorless, gaseous element that burns easily and has less mass than any other element.

hydrosphere (hī′drə sfir), the water portion of the earth.

hygrometer (hī grom′ə tər), an instrument that measures humidity.

hypothesis (hī poth′ə sis), a likely explanation of a problem.

J

jet propulsion (prə pul′shən), a forward motion produced by the reaction of an object to high-pressure gas moving in the opposite direction.

L

lava (lä′və), hot, melted rock that flows from a volcano.

lift (lift), an upward movement.

light zone, the sunlit waters from the ocean surface down to 100 meters.

liquid, a state of matter with a definite volume but no definite shape.

lithosphere (lith′ə sfir), the solid portion of the earth.

low-pressure area, an area where warm air rises and pushes down on the earth with less pressure.

lunar eclipse (lü′nər i klips′), the darkening of the moon as it passes through the earth's shadow.

M

magma (mag′mə), hot, melted rock deep inside the earth.

magma chamber (mag′mə chām′bər), a large, underground lake of magma in the earth's crust.

mantle (man′tl), the earth's middle layer.

mass (mas), the amount of material that an object has in it.

meteor (mē′tē ər), a piece of rock or dust from space burning up in the earth's air.

meteorite (mē′tē ə rīt′), a rock from space that has passed through the air and landed on the ground.

meteorologist (mē′tē ə rol′e jist), a person who studies weather.

mineral (min′ər əl), nonliving solid matter from the earth.

mixture (miks′cher), two or more substances that are placed together but can be easily separated.

molecule (mol′ə kyül), two or more atoms held together.

moraine (mə rān′), a mass or ridge made of rocks, dirt, etc, that were scraped up and deposited by a glacier.

N

nutrient (nü′trē ənt), a material that plants and animals need to live and grow.

O

Oort Cloud, a vast cloud of comets that might exist in space billions of kilometers past the outermost planet.

orbit (ôr′bit), the path of an object around another object.

oxygen (ok′sə jən), a gas that is given off by plants and used by animals.

ozone (ō′zōn) **layer,** the region of concentrated ozone that shields the earth from excessive ultraviolet radiation.

P

pectoral (pek′tər əl) **muscles,** chest muscles.

planet (plan′it), a large body of matter revolving around the sun.

plankton (plangk′tən), the small organisms that float or drift in water, especially at or near the surface.

plate, one of twenty sections of solid rock that make up the earth's crust.

polar climate (pō′lər klī′mit), a major climate zone that receives indirect sunlight all year and that has cold or cool temperatures all year.

pollination (pol′li na′shən), the movement of pollen from a stamen to a pistil.

pollution (pə lü′shən), the addition of harmful substances to land, air, or water.

precipitation (pri sip′ə tā′shən), moisture that falls to the ground from clouds.

pressure (presh′ər), the force exerted on a certain area.

producer (prə dü′sər), a living thing that can use sunlight to make sugars.

property (prop′ər tē), something about an object that can be observed, such as size or shape.

R

rain gauge (gāj), an instrument that measures precipitation.

rainforest, a very dense forest in a region, usually tropical, where rain is very heavy throughout the year.

recycle (rē sī′kəl), to change something so it can be reused.

reef (rēf), narrow ridge of rocks, sand, or coral at or near the surface of the water.

revolution (rev′ə lü′shən), the movement of one object around another object.

rotation (rō tā′shən), one full spin of an object around an axis.

S

saliva (sə lī′və), the fluid in the mouth that makes chewed food wet and begins digestion.

saturated (sach′ə rā′tid) **air,** air that contains all the water vapor it can possibly hold.

season (sē′zn), one of the four periods of the year—spring, summer, fall, or winter.

sedimentary (sed′ə men′tər ē) **rock,** rock made of sediments that have been pressed together.

seismograph (sīz′mə graf), an instrument for recording the direction, strength, and time of earthquakes or other movements of the earth's crust.

solar eclipse (sō′lər i klips′), the blocking of sunlight by the moon as the moon passes between the sun and the earth.

solar system, the sun, the nine planets and their moons, and other objects that orbit the sun.

solid, a state of matter with a definite shape and a definite volume.

solstice (sol′stis), either of the two times in the year when the sun is at its greatest distance from the equator and appears to be farthest north or south in the sky.

solution (sə lü′shən), a mixture in which one substance spreads evenly throughout another substance.

sonic (son′ik) **boom,** a loud noise caused by an airplane crossing through the sound barrier when it travels faster than the speed of sound.

species (spē′shēz), a group of organisms that have the same traits and can produce offspring that can also produce offspring.

star, a ball of hot, glowing gases.

sternum (stėr′nəm), breastbone.

stratus (strā′təs) **cloud,** a cloud that forms in layers that spread across the sky.

subduction (səb′dək shən), the sliding of one of the earth's plates under another.

submersible (səb mėr′sə bəl), that which can be put under water.

subsonic (sub son′ik), having to do with speed less than the speed of sound.

supersonic (sü′pər son′ik), capable of moving faster than sound.

system (sis′təm), a group of organs that work together to do a job; a set of things or parts that form a whole and work together or affect one another.

T

temperate climate (tem′pər it klī′mit), a major climate zone that receives indirect sunlight in the winter and more direct sunlight in the summer.

theory (thē′ər ē), one or more related hypotheses supported by data that best explains things or events.

thermometer (thər mom′ə tər), an instrument for measuring temperature.

thrust (thrust), a forward push.

tremor (trem′ər), a weak earthquake.

trench (trench), a long, narrow valley in the floor of the ocean.

tropical climate (trop′ə kəl klī′mit), a major climate zone that receives direct sunlight and has warm temperatures all year.

V

variable (ver′ē ə bəl), anything in an experiment that can be changed.

volcano (vol kā′nō), a mountain with an opening through which lava, ashes, rocks, and other materials come out.

W

warm front, the area where a warm air mass runs into a cold air mass and slides up over the cold air.

water cycle (sī′kəl), the movement of water by evaporation, condensation, and precipitation.

water molecule (mol′ə kyül), the smallest particle of water.

water vapor (wô′tər vā′pər), water in the form of gas.

weathering (weᴛʜ′ər ing), wearing down or breaking apart rocks.

weight (wāt), force that gravity exerts on a mass.

wind, air that is moving from an area of high pressure to an area of low pressure.

wind vane (vān), a tool that shows wind direction.

Index

Fish
  in caves, B72
  around coral reefs, B71
  in ocean dark zone, B69
  in ocean light zone, B66-68
  parts of, B56-57
Flying (by birds), D21-38
Flying (by machines), D41-56, D58-61
Folded mountains, C44
Food
  Calories in, D28-29
  for flying birds, D28-29
  water and, B50
Food chain, F15
Fossils, C56
Franklin, Benjamin, E20-21
Fresh water, B56-59
Front, E11, E25
  cold, E14-17
  warm, E17, E54
Fuji, Mount, C17
Fungi, F16, F19

G

Gardening, E74-76
  in salt water, B60-61, B63
Gases, A46, D5
  in magma, C9
  on other planets, A26, A27, A33, A36
  solids vs., D9
  in volcanoes, C27
Glaciers, B6, B7, B40-43
Gliders, D42, D43, D54-55
Gliding (by birds), D33
Grand Canyon, B36-37, B44
Granite, B31, C36, C45
Grass, E48-49
Grassland climate, E38, E48-49
Gravity, A8-13, C71, D6
  solar system and, A26
Great Barrier Reef, B70
Great Lakes, B41. *See also* Lake Erie

Great Red Spot, A33
Greenhouse effect, F32-33, F37

H

Halley's comet, A37
Hauk, Terri, C60
Hawaii, C5, C9, E33
  formation of, C13, C14-15, C36
Heat, A24, A28, E28
  See also Energy; Temperature
Helicopters, D61
Helium, A26, A33
Highland climate, E39, E47
Homo sapiens, A53
Hot spots, C13, C14-15
How Things Work
  helicopter, D61
  iron from ore, extracting, C61
  microbursts and airplanes, E77
  pollination, F61
  Remotely Operated Vehicle, B77
  space suit, A61
Human body
  wastes of, B50, B51
  water in, B48
  water and, B47-48, B50-51
Humid continental climate, E39, E45
Humidity, E5-6, E9, E32
  air masses and, E10
  measuring, E60, E62, E70-71
Humid subtropical climate, E39, E44
Hummingbird, D35, D61, F61
Hurricanes, E67-69
Hydrosphere, A44-47
Hygrometer, E60, E62

I

Ice, B5-7, B16-17
  formation of, B9
  rocks changed by, B29-31.
  See also Erosion
Iceberg, B16
Ice crystals, E7, E54

O

Obsidian, C36
Ocean floor, C36, C47
Oceans, A51, A53
    climate and, E40-41
    erosion and, B39
    as habitats, B62-71
    pollution of, B76
    See also Beaches; Pacific Ocean
Oort Cloud, A37
Orbit
    of comets, A37
    of Earth, A5, A7, E30, E35-36
    gravity and, A13
    of moon, A10, A18
    of Pluto, A37
    See also Rotation
Orchids, F18
Ore, C61
Oxygen
    in atmosphere, A44, D6, D9, F36
    digestive system and, B50
    in mantle of earth, C6
    plants and, F12-13
Ozone layer, D6-7, D53

P

Pacific Ocean, B65-71
Perspiration (sweat), B51, E5, E6
Pinatubo, Mount, C27
Planet, Earth as a, A5
Planets, A5, A25-40
    names of, A37
    temperature of, A30-31
    See also Solar system
Plankton, A50, A51, B66, B69

Plants
    as colonizers, C33
    extinct, F34-35
    used for medicine, F34, F35
    in rainforest, F10, F15-19
    saltwater, B60
    as survivors, C31
    water and, A49, A50-53, B49, B52-53
    See also Gardening; Seeds; Vegetables
Plates, C12-13
    earthquakes and, C45, C48-55
    mountains and, C44-45, C46-47
    subduction of, C17
Pluto, A25, A34, A36-37
Polar climate, E33
Pollination, F17, F61
Pollution, B24-25, B76
Ponds, A49, B58-59
Prairie dogs, E49
Prairies, E48
Pressure
    of air, D8-9
    earthquakes and, C49
    magma and, C8, C27
Propellers, D43, D45, D48-49
Pumice, C36
Puu Oo, Mount, C9

Q

Quartz, B31
Quetzal, F58-59

R

Radar weather reports, E62, E66, E77
Rain, A47
    air masses and, E12
    amount of, B21
    climate zones and, E38-39
    clouds predicting, E54, E55
    cold fronts and, E14
    erosion and, B34
    formation of, B9, E7
    rocks and, B30-31

Acknowledgments

ScottForesman

Editorial: Terry Flohr, Janet Helenthal, Mary Ann Mortellaro, Kathleen Ludwig, Glen Phelan, Matthew Shimkus

Art and Design: Barbara Schneider, Jacqueline Kolb, George Roth, Cathy Sterrett

Picture Research/Photo Studio: Nina Page, Kelly Mountain, Judy Ladendorf, John Moore

Photo Lab/Keyline: Marilyn Sullivan, Mark Barberis, Gwen Plogman

Production: Barbara Albright, Francine Simon

Marketing: Lesa Scott, Ed Rock

Ligature, Inc.

Pupil Edition interior design and production

Unless otherwise acknowledged, all photographs are the property of ScottForesman. Unless otherwise acknowledged, all computer graphics by Ligature, Inc. Page abbreviations are as follows: **(T)** top, **(C)** center, **(B)** bottom, **(L)** left, **(R)** right, **(INS)** inset.

Module A
Photographs
Front & Back Cover: Background: "Constellations of the Northern Hemisphere" chart © Frank Schaffer Co., Frank Schaffer Publications Inc.   Children's Photos: John Moore

Page A2,16,17,22,26,27,28,29,32,33,36,43,59(TL-INS), 60 NASA   **A3(T)** Jon Riley/Tony Stone Worldwide   **A18,19(T)** A Mount Wilson & Palomar Observatory Photograph   **A21(L)** National Optical Astronomy Observatories   **A21(R)** National Optical Astronomy Observatories   **A44-45(T)** Jon Riley/Tony Stone Worldwide   **A44-45(C)** Robin Smith/Tony Stone Worldwide   **A44-45(B)** Baron Wolman   **A46** Jeff Schultz/Alaska Photo/All Stock   **A50(ALL)** William H. Amos   **A51** Anne Wertheim/ANIMALS ANIMALS   **A53(T)** Don & Pat Valenti/f/Stop Pictures, Inc.   **A53(B)** Patrice Ceisel/Tom Stack & Associates   **A58** Courtesy of Stuart Elementary School, Patrick County, Virginia   **A59** Park Seed Company   **A59(TL)** NASA   **A62(L)** Don & Pat Valenti/f/Stop Pictures, Inc.   **A62(C)** Don and Pat Valenti   **A62(R)** Don & Pat Valenti/f/Stop Pictures, Inc.

Illustrations
Page A5 Roberta Polfus   **A6-7** Roberta Polfus   **A10-11** Roberta Polfus   **A18-19** George Kelvin   **A34-35** Jacque Auger   **A34-35(INS)** Randy Verougstraete   **A36** Jacque Auger   **A40** Nancy Lee Walter   **A44** Roberta Polfus

Module B
Photographs
Front & Back Cover: Background: Paul Berger/Tony Stone Worldwide   Children's Photos: John Moore

Page B5 E.R.Degginger   **B6-7** Mark Kelly/Alaska Stock Photo   **B8(T)** Wolfgang Kaehler   **B13(R)** Hermann Eisenbeiss/Photo Researchers   **B16(B)** Wolfgang Kaehler   **B24** Robert W. Blickensderfer/Ohio Sea Grant   **B25** Robert W.Blickensderfer   **B30(R)** Ray Pfortner/Peter Arnold, Inc.   **B35(L)** Photo Researchers   **B36-37** Francois Gohier/Photo Researchers   **B38(R)** Jack Dermid/Photo Researchers   **B39(L)** Scott Blackman/Tom Stack & Associates   **B40-41** Robert C. Fields/Earth Scenes   **B44-45** Baron Wolman   **B48** E.R.Degginger   **B51(L)** From BEHOLD MAN/Lennart Nilsson/Bonnier Fakta   **B51(R)** Steve Allen/Peter Arnold, Inc.   **B54-55** Carl Purcell/Photo Researchers   **B58** Visuals Unlimited   **B59** Zig Leszczynski/ANIMALS ANIMALS   **B62(L)** Andrew J.Martinez   **B62(R)** Stephen Frink/Waterhouse   **B69** Bruce Robinson   **B70(L)** Andrew J. Martinez   **B70-71** Fred Bavendam/Peter Arnold, Inc.   **B71(INS)** Andrew J.Martinez   **B72** Visuals Unlimited   **B75** Visuals Unlimited   **B76** Will Brown for ScottForesman

Illustrations
Page B22-23 Joe Le Monnier   **B35** Charles Thomas   **B37** Joe Le Monnier   **B38** Walter Stuart   **B44** JAK Graphics   **B56-57** Walter Stuart   **B58-59** Cindy Brodie   **B65** Walter Stuart   **B67** Walter Stuart   **B68** Walter Stuart   **B77** George Kelvin

Module C
Photographs
Front & Back Cover: Background: Visuals Unlimited   Children's Photos: John Moore

Page C3(TL) Reuters/UPI/Bettmann   **C3(B)** Paul Miller/Black Star   **C5(T)** Dave Millert/Tom Stack & Associates   **C5(B)** Visuals Unlimited   **C7(T)** Ron Watts/Black Star   **C14** Michael and Patricia Fogden   **C19** E.R.Degginger   **C22(CR)** Stephen Dalton/Photo Researchers   **C25** Gary Braasch   **C25(INS)** David Olson/Black Star   **C27** Reuters/UPI/Bettmann   **C30** Peter Frenzen/U.S.Forestry Service   **C31(BL)** Jerry Franklin/U.S.Forestry Service   **C32** Gary Braasch   **C32(INS)** Gary Braasch   **C34-35** David Olson/Black Star   **C34(TC)** Thomas Kitchin/Tom Stack & Associates   **C34(BC)** Gary Braasch   **C35(TC)** Peter K.Ziminski/Visuals Unlimited   **C35(BR)** Gary Braasch   **C36(C)** Tim Rock/Earth Scenes   **C36(B)** Anna E. Zuckerman/ Tom Stack & Associates   **C40** William H.Amos   **C43** Reprinted Courtesy of H.M.Gousha/Simon & Schuster   **C44** Visuals Unlimited   **C45** Visuals Unlimited   **C48** David Olson/Black Star   **C49** Paul Miller/Black Star   **C49(INS)** Arnold Genthe/Library of Congress   **C52(T)** NASA   **C58** Alfred Borcover   **C60** James E.Stoots, Jr./Lawrence Livermore National Laboratory

Illustrations
Page C2 Ebet Dudley   **C7** Ebet Dudley   **C8-9** Ebet Dudley
C12-13 Ebet Dudley   **C14-15** Joe Le Monnier   **C16-17** Joe Le
Monnier   **C18** Joe Le Monnier   **C18(INS)** Ebet Dudley
C22 Ebet Dudley   **C44-45** Ebet Dudley   **C48** Ebet Dudley
C50-51 Hank Iken   **C56** JAK Graphics   **C59** Rich Lo
C61 Rich Lo

Module D
Photographs
Front & Back Cover: Background: Kim Taylor/Bruce Coleman,
Inc.   Children's Photos: John Moore

Page D3(ALL T) Stephen Dalton/Photo Researchers
D3(BL) The Granger Collection, New York   **D5** Michael &
Patricia Fogden   **D21** Stephen Dalton/ANIMALS ANIMALS
D22(L) Stephen Dalton/Photo Researchers   **D24(L)** NOAA/
NESDIS/NCDC   **D24(R)** T.C.Kelley/Photo Researchers
D26-27 Tom McHugh/Photo Researchers   **D28** Kim Taylor/
Bruce Coleman, Inc.   **D32(T)** Frans Lanting/Minden Pictures
D34(L) Wendy Shattil and Bob Rozinski/Tom Stack & Associates
D35(B) Francois Gohier/Photo Researchers   **D38** Pat & Tom
Leeson/Photo Researchers   **D40** Richard Legeckis/Nesdid/
Rsmas/NOAA/NESDIS/NCDC   **D41** The Granger Collection,
New York   **D42(T)** Science Museum, London   **D44(T)** Greg
Vaughn/Tom Stack & Associates   **D44(B)** Haward Gallery
London, Tetva Associates   **D45(CR)** NASA   **D45(TC)** Library
of Congress   **D45(BC)** Library of Congress   **D50(T)** John
Covant/Photri, Inc.   **D52** NASA   **D53** NASA
D58(T) AP/Wide World   **D58(B)** M Barrett/H. Armstrong
Roberts   **D62(L)** Rod Planck/Tom Stack & Associates
D62(C) Stephen Dalton/ANIMALS ANIMALS
D62(R) Frans Lanting/ALLSTOCK,INC.
D67(ALL) E/NOAA/NESDIS/NCDC

Illustrations
Page D5 Toni Goffe   **D6-7** Francisco Maruca
D8(T) Francisco Maruca   **D8(B)** Toni Goffe   **D24-25** Eric
Wright   **D28** Dickson O. Tabe   **D32-33** Kirk Caldwell
D34 Kirk Caldwell   **D35** Kirk Caldwell   **D42-43** Chris
Costello   **D50-51** Chris Costello   **D56** JAK Graphics
D58 JAK Graphics

Module E
Photographs
Front Cover: Children's Photos: John Moore

Page E3(TL) NOAA   **E3(TR)** Van Bucher/Photo Researchers
E3(B) Franca Principe, Instituto e Museo di Storra della Scienza,
Florence   **E15** Warren Faidley/Weatherstock   **E16** Wolfgang
Kaehler   **E22** Michael & Elvan Habicht/Earth Scenes
E23 Elvan Habicht/Peter Arnold, Inc.   **E24(L)** NOAA/NESDIS/
NCDC   **E29(L)** G.I.Bernard/Earth Scenes   **E29(R)** G.I.Bernard/
Earth Scenes   **E30(T)** James P. Jackson/Photo Researchers
E31 Gary Braasch/Alaska Photo Collection/ALLSTOCK
E37(L) Charlie Ott/Photo Researchers   **E37(R)** E.R.Degginger
E41 ERIM, Ann Arbor, MI   **E45** Richard Kolar/Earth Scenes
E46 Peter B.Kaplan/Photo Researchers   **E47(R)** Peter B.Kaplan/
Photo Researchers   **E48(T)** Mickey Gibson/Earth Scenes
E48(B) Peter Arnold, Inc.   **E49** Peter Arnold, Inc.
E50 E.R.Degginger   **E53** E.R.Degginger   **E54(T)** Bob
Daemmrich/Stock Boston   **E54(T INS)** Joyce Photographics/
Photo Researchers   **E54(B)** Richard Pasley/Stock Boston
E54(B INS) E.R.Degginger   **E55(T)** David Woodward/Tony
Stone Worldwide   **E55(T INS)** Gary Brettnacher/Tony Stone
Worldwide   **E55(B)** Sam C.Pierson/Photo Researchers

E55(B INS) Tony Freeman/Photo Edit   **E58** E.R.Degginger
E60 Franca Principe, Instituto e Museo di Storia della Scienza,
Florence   **E61** Van Bucher/Photo Researchers   **E62(T)** Photo
Researchers   **E62(B)** Stephen Frisch/Stock Boston   **E63** Tony
Stone Worldwide   **E75** E.R.Degginger

Illustrations
Page E11 Joe Le Monnier   **E12-13** Joe Le Monnier
E14 Joe Le Monnier   **E17** Joe Le Monnier   **E32** Susan Nethery
E36-37 Greg McNair   **E38-39** Joe Le Monnier   **E57** Susan
Nethery   **E72** JAK Graphics   **E77** Gary Torrisi

Module F
Photographs
Front & Back Cover: Background: Victor Englebert   Children's
Photos: John Moore

Page F2(BR) Michael & Patricia Fogden   **F6** Victor Englebert
F14(T) Michael & Patricia Fogden   **F14(C)** Michael & Patricia
Fogden   **F14(B)** Jany Sauvamet/Photo Researchers
F19(L) Gary Retherford/Photo Researchers
F19(C) Jack Swenson/Tom Stack & Associates
F19(R) J.P. Varin/Jacana/Tom Stack & Associates
F24(C) NOAA/NESDIS/NCDC   **F25(L)** Rugerio Reis/Black
Star   **F25(R)** Walt Anderson/Visuals Unlimited   **F26** Victor
Englebert   **F28** Dan Brennan/Knut Bry   **F30(B)** Loren McIntyre
F40 John Cancalosi/Peter Arnold, Inc.   **F44(T)** Jane Thomas/
Visuals Unlimited   **F44(B)** Loren McIntyre   **F45(T)** Victor
Englebert   **F45(B)** George Loun/Visuals Unlimited
F59(T) E.R.Degginger   **F59(B)** Michael Fogden/Bruce Coleman,
Inc.   **F60** Courtesy University of Wisconsin

Illustrations
Page F3 John Burgoyne   **F7** Mark Smith   **F8-9** Cindy Brodie
F10 John Burgoyne   **F14-15** John Burgoyne   **F28-29** Joe Le
Monnier   **F30** Joe Le Monnier   **F34-35** Wild Onion Studio
F36 Ebet Dudley   **F56** JAK Graphics   **F61** Wild Onion Studio
Leaf Borders throughout module (**F4, 5, 6, 7, 10, 11, 14, 16, 17,
18, 19, 24, 25, 28, 29, 30, 31, 34, 35, 42, 43, 46, 47, 50, 51,
52, 53**) by John Burgoyne